SECRETS AND TRUTHS

The Natalie Zemon Davis Annual Lecture Series
at Central European University, Budapest

SECRETS AND TRUTHS:
ETHNOGRAPHY
IN THE ARCHIVE OF
ROMANIA'S SECRET POLICE

Katherine Verdery

Central European University Press

Budapest – New York

© 2014 by Katherine Verdery

Published in 2014 by
Central European University Press
An imprint of the Central European University Limited Liability Company
Nádor utca 11, H-1051 Budapest, Hungary
Tel: +36-1-327-3138 or 327-3000 · *Fax:* +36-1-327-3183
E-mail: ceupress@ceu.hu · Website: www.ceupress.com

224 West 57th Street, New York NY 10019, USA
Tel: +1-212-547-6932 · *Fax:* +1-646-557-2416
E-mail: martin.greenwald@opensocietyfoundations.org

Series design by Péter Tóth

ISBN 978-615-5225-99-4
ISSN 1996-1197

Library of Congress Cataloging-in-Publication Data
Verdery, Katherine, 1948
  Secrets and truths : ethnography in the archive of Romania's secret police /
Katherine Verdery.
      pages cm
  Includes bibliographical references and index.
  ISBN 978 6155225994
  1. Romania. Securitatea. 2. Secret service—Romania History. 3. Political
persecution—Romania—History. I. Title.

  HV8241.8.A45S439 2014
  363.28'309498—dc23

                                    2013029653

Printed in Hungary by Prime Rate Kft., Budapest

Familiei mele din satul Aurel Vlaicu, cu mult drag

Meri și Sîvu
Moașa și Moșu
Angela, Florin, și Ani

To my family in the village of Aurel Vlaicu, with much love

Table of Contents

List of Figures

ix

Preface and Acknowledgments

The end of Soviet-style socialism brought into public awareness a set of archives whose makers had never imagined that they would be revealed: the archives of the communist-era secret police in Eastern Europe. The archives soon entered into the political process of "decommunization," used to prove whether one or another citizen had collaborated with the police and might thus be unsuitable for public office in a postsocialist polity. Made accessible to varying degrees in the formerly socialist countries, the archives also attracted researchers eager to explore these extraordinary sources in order to understand better the workings of socialism. A third use emerged as well: in some countries, people who had been the objects of surveillance could see their own files, to generally painful effect.

Each of these purposes—political, research, and personal—involved potential revisions of history in the service of a transformed present. For all three purposes, questions of the truth-value of the archives' contents were paramount. If a person's name appears in the registry of collaborators, had he really collaborated? If a name is missing from the registry, does that confirm innocence? Were officers' reports credible representations of how the organization really worked? Were the archives complete, or had important sections of them been destroyed? Those and many other questions ricochet around the space opened by this newly available source, whose very newness makes the questions uncommonly difficult to answer. Users of these archives are pioneers with little precedent to guide them.

The recency of my own approach to them makes my arguments in this book somewhat tentative. I first encountered the Romanian secret police (Securitate) archive while researching a book on the collectivization of Romanian agriculture,[1] for which the archive provided some useful information about villagers' experiences. At the encouragement of one of the archivists, I eventually requested my own surveillance file and entered more fully into the archive; I also began to read about intelligence services elsewhere in the Soviet bloc. Having barely embarked on this work when I received the invitation to deliver the Natalie Zemon Davis lectures in Budapest, I decided to use the occasion to explore what an ethnographic approach to this archive might look like and how one might think about questions of its truth-value. The lectures present some initial moments in such thinking. Only the press's publication schedule for the lecture series has induced me to release them at this point.

When I received Gábor Klaniczay's kind invitation to deliver them, I wondered how an East Europeanist anthropologist (unlike all my predecessors in this lecture series, who have been primarily West European historians) could say anything appropriate in honor of Professor Natalie Davis—especially since my research goes back only to the 1950s, unlike my predecessors, who were nearly all medievalists or early-modernists. What connections might I have with the rich and informative corpus of work she has offered us? It is a sign of her breadth and virtuosity that even someone like me can find many points of intersection. Let me indicate three, having to do with theme, with historical period, and with personal history.

First, in her famous *Fiction in the Archives*, Professor Davis showed how much you can do with documents, well beyond their "truth-value"—a particularly helpful lesson for the source I will explore in these lectures, whose truth-value is deeply in question. Moreover, among the persistent themes she has explored has been that of imposture, assumed identity, and disguise. She has a fondness for the idea of the trickster, that staple of Native American ethnography, who escapes obligation by assuming different identities.[2] Her best-known work of this kind was *The Return of Martin Guerre;* her *Remaking Imposters: From Martin Guerre to Sommersby* takes it up as well, as does her book *Trickster Travels*, which describes how a sixteenth-century Muslim lived as a Christian in Italy. This theme of disguise is central to my source, as I have had ample opportunity to see from my surveillance records from 1973 to 1989 (during which I had spent about three years conducting research in Romania). The Securitate's fundamental working assumption was that *people are not who they seem*; its job, like that of all the services spawned by the KGB—of all intelligence services, for that matter—, was to find out *who people really were*. (In my case, they sought evidence that I was not a scholar but a spy, and from their point of view they found plenty of it.)

My second link to Natalie Davis's *oeuvre* comes from early modern France, the site of so much of her research. Among my favorite books about Soviet-style socialism is *The Dissolution of Communist Power*, by Hungarian scholars Ágnes Horváth and Árpád Szakolczai. Synthesizing their work on mid-level Party activists in Hungary, they ask about the nature of the power that the Communist Party apparatus exercised, and they find their answer in the governmental technology invented by the early modern police of Europe's absolutist states.[3] We know that the police organization of early modern France, in particular, influenced the development of policing in tsarist Russia; that, in turn, provided the model for the Bolshevik police culminating in the KGB, who passed many features of it along to the security services of Eastern Europe. So I join Natalie Davis from an unexpected angle, as I speak about not only fictions and disguise but the heirs of early modern French policing.

There is a third, much more personal link between my subject and Natalie Davis's life. During the so-called Red Scare in the US in the 1950s, she and her husband, Chandler Davis (who was a member of the American Communist Party until 1953), were harassed for refusing to cooperate with the House Un-American Activities Committee in its pursuit of "communist sympathizers." In consequence, he was fired from his position at the University of Michigan and sentenced to six months in jail, and their passports were confiscated, cutting her off from her archival research for eight years. He eventually found a teaching job in Canada, at the University of Toronto. So Natalie Davis knows a great deal more than most Americans about surveillance and the fear tactics that accompanied the Cold War. I salute the courage she and her husband demonstrated then, in circumstances all too familiar to many of the people harassed by Eastern Europe's secret police.

I am exceedingly grateful for the help of a number of people who offered comment on one or another part of this project, both in Budapest at the time of the lectures and during their preparation. My first debt is to Virgiliu Țârău, Florica Dobre, Cristina Anisescu, and their colleagues at the National Council for the Study of the Securitate Archives (CNSAS) in Bucharest, for the remarkable degree of support they provided during my several visits there, as well as by email. Maya Nadkarni, Florin Poenaru, Anikó Szűcs, and Cristina Vatulescu responded generously to endless questions and gave extended comment on the manuscript. I enjoyed the further assistance of Andrew Abbott, Nadia Al-Bagdadi, Sorin Antohi, Margaret Beissinger, John Borneman, Liviu Chelcea, William Christian, Silvia Colfescu, Natalie Davis, Dennis Deletant, Andreas Glaeser, Saygun Gökarıksel, Bruce Grant, Jan Gross, Irina Grudzinska-Gross, Lynn Hunt, William Kelly, Gábor Klaniczay, Gail Kligman, Stephen Kotkin, Mária Kovács, Ioana Macrea-Toma, Oana Mateescu, Silviu Moldovan, Vlad Naumescu, Marius Oprea, Serguei Oushakine, István Rév, Alfred Rieber, Marsha Siefert, and Marilyn Strathern. An early version of chapter 3 was presented at the Geisteswissen-schaftliche Zentrum Geschichte und Kultur Ostmit-teleuropas (GWZO) at the University of Leipzig, as the Oscar Halecki Lecture for 2010. My thanks to Prof. Dr. Christian Lübke and Dr. Dietmar Müller for their comments and assistance on that occasion. I am deeply indebted to Nóra Vörös for her outstand-ing work in bringing the book to press.

A research grant at Princeton University's Shelby Cullum Davis Center for Historical Studies (fall 2010) nurtured my writing. I gained immensely from the companionship and thoughtful commentary of my fel-low scholars: Monica Black, Yair Mintzker, Mary Mor-gan, Mridu Rai, Dan Rodgers, Hugh Thomas, and Eric Weitz. Funds provided by the National Council for Eurasian and East European Research (NCEEER) through a Title VIII grant from the US Department of State supported a portion of the research, though nei-ther NCEEER nor the US government is responsible for the views I express. Additional research funds came from the City University of New York Graduate Cen-ter. My thanks to all these sources of support.

Finally, Phyllis Mack not only put up with the in-cursions of yet another writing project into our life but read the lectures in multiple drafts, offering her cus-tomary incisive yet warm and encouraging response. I thank her, especially.

Note on Pronunciation

Romanian is pronounced more or less like Italian, with the following additions:

ă = like the *u* in *but* [schwa]

î (also â) = a high central vowel with no English equivalent; the final *e* in *intelligent*, spoken quickly, approximates it.

ş = *sh* as in *shoe*

ţ = *ts* as in *fits*

Final *i* is often not pronounced, becoming voiceless and/or palatalizing the preceding consonant. Before another vowel, *i* usually becomes a glide (thus, Ion = Yon)

As in Italian, front vowels soften *c* and *g* (to č and dj); hard *c* or *g* before front vowels is spelled *ch* or *gh*.

Word stress varies but tends toward the penultimate.

For purposes of this book:

Securitate, seh-coo-ree-TAH-teh or (with the definite article) Securitatea, seh-coo-ree-TAH-teh-ah.

Securitate officers were popularly referred to as Securişti (seh-coo-REESHT'), singular Securist (seh-coo-REEST), or Secu (SEH-coo), for short.

All translations from the Romanian are mine, except where otherwise noted.

xix

Introduction

What Was the Securitate?

God preserve me from those who want
what's best for me,
the nice guys
always ready to inform on me cheerfully.
From the priest with a tape-recorder under his vestment
and the blanket you can't get under without saying
Good evening.

—Mircea Dinescu, "Cold Comfort"[1]

Following the disestablishment of Communist Party rule in the Soviet bloc, political pressure arose in nearly every East European country to cleanse the polity of legacies of the prior regime. Former Party officials were to be banned from office, as was anyone known to have collaborated with communist power, especially with the secret police. These demands partook of a broader world movement for so-called transitional justice, by which citizens of successor states to dictatorships of various kinds sought to address and overcome their countries' repressive pasts. Applied to cases as varied as South Africa, Rwanda, Argentina, and Chile as well as the former Soviet sphere, transitional

1

justice concerned such questions as how to exit from authoritarianism into democracy and the rule of law; how to bring the perpetrators of human rights violations to justice and compensate their victims; how to prevent supporters of the prior regime from corrupting or destabilizing the new order; how to reconcile warring parties; and how to come to terms with deeply troubling histories and rewrite national narratives.

In the former Soviet bloc, these processes took an idiosyncratic form, focused on the archives of the communist secret police. Beginning with Czechoslovakia and Germany in 1990-91, laws were passed requiring that aspirants to political office and certain other posts be vetted through the secret police archive, to prove that they had not served as collaborators. This practice, often known as "lustration" (from the Czech *lustrace*), spread throughout the region to varying degrees over the subsequent two decades.[2] With it emerged numerous disputes concerning the contents of the archives and their suitability for the purposes to which they were being put. The media in nearly every country of the region became saturated with informer scandals, debates over the truth-value of the secret police files, arguments about whether transitional justice was being properly accomplished, and other such concerns.[3] Many citizens in Eastern Europe gained access to their files and experienced the shock of discovering that their best friends or spouses had informed on them. Accusations and denials followed.

In Hungary alone, a very partial reckoning gives us the Péter Medgyessy scandal, the István Szabó scandal, the Imre Mécs Commission, the libel suits against historian Krisztián Ungváry, the László Kiss affair, Péter Esterházy's painful reflections in *Javított kiadás (Revised Edition)* on his revered father's collaboration, and so on.[4] In 2010, the Orbán government proposed dismantling the secret police archive by simply letting everyone take their own file home. Hungarians' concern with secret police files was evident even in the US, where an article on the topic by celebrated historian István Deák appeared in the *New York Review of Books* in 2006 and journalist Kati Marton published her *Enemies of the People*, based on her parents' Hungarian secret police files.[5] Comparable lists could easily be drawn up for other East European countries.

The "file fever" spreading throughout the region affected me as well. Following my initial research in the Securitate archive from 2000 to 2006, I requested and received multiple volumes of my own surveillance file, some 2,780 pages altogether (the product of over three years of research in Romania between 1973 and 1989).[6] Only then did I start to think about making the archive itself my object. Aside from studying my file, I have consulted a number of others in the

3

archive and read portions of still others in published form,[7] but mountains of yet-unread books and archival material remain.

Contrary to the emphases I listed above, I am not concerned except in a tangential way with the issues that have motivated much of the writing on this topic: governmental transparency, democratization, matters of transitional justice, informer scandals, or the truth-value of the secret police files. My goal in thinking about Securitate files in general and my own in particular is to shed light on the lives of these files and to ask what they and their contents tell us that we did not already know about the socialist system, or at least knew less clearly than we might now. That is, I am not as interested in reasserting often-made arguments about how bad the Securitate was—though I fully agree that it did devastating harm to many people, and it should be condemned for that fact—as in examining less-obvious aspects of their methods and work habits, aspects unavailable to us before this archive was opened. I hope additionally to contribute to an ethnography of the socialist state by inquiring into its relationship to people it defined as "external enemies," like me, whom it nevertheless invited in.

Readers might ask what a scholar from the US can bring to this subject, as compared with citizens of Eastern Europe, and how I can justify speaking of it when others suffered so much more than I from the communist secret police. Although I indeed suffered less than many others, my entire professional and much of my emotional life for forty years has been devoted to Romania, starting with my doctoral research in 1973 and continuing with repeated visits thereafter. Throughout my research, my collegial relations and friendships deepened, and like many anthropologists, I was "adopted" into quasi-kinship roles (as my book's dedication shows). Going through my file and discovering who among my associates reported on me has not been easy.[8] Perhaps my way of trying to think about it will prove illuminating to others, as I have sought to move beyond outrage by treating my file as an ethnographic object.[9]

This is part of what I mean by my subtitle, "ethnography in the archive." What else do I mean by it? One of my discipline's most accomplished practitioners of this art, Ann Stoler, treats the archive not as a source but as a site of knowledge production and concept formation, a repository of and generator of social relationships. She inspects colonial documents for the conceptual labor they reveal, the epistemologies that underpin them.[10] Although I aspire to many of her goals, mine at this stage in my research must be more modest. My ethnographic venture here includes bringing some anthropological literature to bear on

5

my topic, as in my second chapter concerning secrets and secret societies, and also making use of myself—a classic move for ethnographers, whose central research instrument is themselves, above all.

For example, a 1985 Securitate report concludes that I undoubtedly have intelligence experience because in writing my fieldnotes I use a special code; I call the people I speak with "informers" and give them "conspiratorial names"; I always give the context and location of a discussion, the informer's attitude, and my own questions; I keep taking fieldnotes on things well outside the limits of my research proposal, indicating something suspicious; in writing my notes I use a special code and I take them all to the US Embassy, keeping none to use in writing my book, as would be normal; and I am preoccupied with learning the identity of Securitate informers among my contacts.[11] Reading this was a revelation, for I could see their point. Were they right: *was* I a spy?[12] Were *Securiști* (Securitate officers) and I doing the same thing? I didn't think so; I started out as a lowly graduate student who barely spoke the language—not very promising spy material—but it was true that I referred to people I interviewed as "informants"[13] and created pseudonyms for them in my fieldnotes; I used a form of shorthand to speed up my note-taking; and to protect people I spoke with I mailed out all my cop-

6

ies through the US Embassy diplomatic pouch rather than keeping a copy at hand. Beyond this, as an ethnographer I was trained not just to pursue a narrow project but to be interested in everything and to contextualize all the information I obtained. And I shared this very broad investigative strategy with the Securitate, for whom "ethnography" in the Romanian tradition meant teams making brief research trips to collect folklore, not living for months on end in a village as I was doing. In my behavior they recognized their own, forcing me now to consider the parallels between theirs and mine. To be an ethnographer in this archive, then, means being forced to question the premises of one's own practice.

The questions work both ways. Just as Natalie Davis opened *The Return of Martin Guerre* by saying, "This book grew out of a historian's adventure with a different way of telling things about the past,"[14] my work has grown out of an anthropologist's adventure with a different way of doing ethnography. For that is what the Securitate did: make close examinations of everyday behavior and interpret what they found. That they employed a specific interpretive lens for what they gathered does not distinguish them from most other practitioners of the ethnographic method. Therefore, I seek to understand the police as ethnographers, to ask about their techniques

7

for getting beneath the "disguises" of those they followed, to inspect their categories of thought and the kind of knowledge they tried to create. How did Securitate agents do what they did, and what can ethnography in their archive tell us about it? In pursuing these questions I follow and incorporate the work of a new generation of outstanding scholars such as Andreas Glaeser, for East Germany; Anikó Szűcs and Maya Nadkarni, for Hungary; Saygun Gökarıksel, for Poland; and Cristina Anisescu, Florin Poenaru, and Cristina Vatulescu, for Romania.[15]

In the remainder of this Introduction I offer some background on the Securitate, necessary for the chapters that follow. I will give a brief history of it, place it in the landscape of Romanian governmental organizations, and outline the theory of power that undergirded it.

What Was the Securitate?[16]

During and after World War II, all the intelligence services in Eastern Europe were created under close Soviet guidance.[17] The specific institutional arrangements of these organizations differed from one country to another, in part according to the degree of confidence the Soviets placed in the Communist leadership of the various East European parties. In the case of Romania, that confidence was near zero. The Romanian Communist Party (RCP), banned since 1924, was among the region's weakest, numbering only about one thousand members at the end of the war. Given the Party's high level of factionalism and low appeal among the populace, Party leaders could remain in power only with extensive Soviet assistance—and with that came constant monitoring by the secret police, which the Soviets would have to control. We see the Soviet leadership's utter distrust of the RCP leadership in the instruction given by Romania's Interior Minister (he was a Soviet NKVD officer) to place microphones secretly in the home and office of Party leader Gheorghiu-Dej, on orders from Moscow.

The Securitate was formed as such in 1948, as the Direcția Generală a Securității Poporului (General Directorate of the People's Security), having as its aim "the defense of the democratic achievements, the guarantee of the security of the Romanian People's Republic, against the machinations of enemies from within and without."[18] It eventually became one of the largest East European intelligence services, proportional to population. The Soviet NKVD/KGB[19] was instrumental in its formation: its first Director, as well as several of its deputies and other top officials, were Soviet NKVD officers, and Soviet coun-

9

cilors continued to advise the Romanian Communist Party about intelligence matters until they were finally sent home in 1964. Romanian political scientist Stelian Tănase has argued that the Securitate was consolidated as an organization by the campaign to verify Party members that occurred under KGB supervision between 1948 and 1950; it resulted in purging almost a third of the Party membership, which had quickly grown from about one thousand in 1944 to over one million in 1948.[20]

I note two caveats to these comments about Soviet influence. First, many Romanian commentators on the Securitate (particularly its actions up to 1964) tend to overstress that influence, as part of proving that the organization's most malevolent acts were committed by others, not by Romanians—an evidently tendentious claim.[21] Second, it is important to emphasize that the Securitate took shape on the back, and with some of the personnel, of several interwar intelligence services, including the Siguranţa and the related Special Information Service. To a degree, those earlier organizations may have shared some techniques with the KGB, as is suggested by documents in the Romanian archives of the 1930s that show a security police asking questions and using terms very similar to those found in the Securitate archive.[22] When the Romanian national state was formed between 1859 and 1871, its founders may have borrowed these along with other features of the French state that they (like certain Russian czars) so admired. The first postal service director, for instance, was a Belgian who learned from France his methods of censoring correspondence.[23]

Because the Securitate kept some of the older intelligence staff, its organizational formulas were less indebted to the KGB than they might otherwise have been, for those cadres were already used to doing things and organizing their work in certain ways that were difficult to adapt to the Soviet model. Moreover, the Soviets could not supply sufficient numbers of councilors to shape things in detail but had to rest with shaping policy and personnel at the upper levels, in hopes that this would staunch some of the osmosis from the older Romanian institutions.[24] An area of struggle between the different organizations concerned the use of informers. The older services had made extensive use of them—a practice partly inspired by a small budget—, its officers keeping informer data only in their memories. (For this reason, according to a publication of the post-Securitate information services, the informers of the older services were never uncovered.[25]) But the new Soviet-inspired Securitate emphasized instead the creation of informers' *files*, which made them easier to penetrate.[26] This

Figure 0.1. The CNSAS archive

not only produced excessive bureaucratic work but was, as Troncotă reports, "a true disaster for preserving the confidentiality of secret human sources. And this is because, as the history of secret services shows well, bureaucracy in work with agents means infinite possibilities for information to trickle out."[27] Happily for us, however, the burgeoning paper trail provides our database for ethnography in this archive.

From 1948 onward, the Securitate underwent several changes in its name, its organizational location, and its status—affecting its degree of autonomy from or integration into the Ministry of the Interior, for instance, its degree of oversight by the NKVD, and its relative independence of the Romanian Communist Party. Over time, it became less closely tied to the Soviet Union than were most of the other East European intelligence services and sought greater cooperation with China—part of Romanian leaders' effort to create greater independence for Romania within the east bloc.[28] Toward this end, as of the early 1960s Romania began to remove Securitate officers trained in the Soviet Union, purging 70–80 percent of cadres of Ukrainian, Russian, or Jewish nationality and those with Russian wives. In 1964 Party leaders issued the "April Declaration," refusing a number of Soviet plans that would have subordinated the country within a Soviet-dictated division of labor, which included dismantling schools for espionage training in the East European countries. From then on, cooperation between the Securitate and the other secret services dropped off; Troncotă cites a memo sent by the KGB to Czech Party leaders, asking them not to give the Romanians certain kinds of information.[29] Securitate cadres ceased to be formed in the KGB academy and officers were no longer sent there for specialization, unlike all the other communist security services (indeed, Hungary, Czechoslovakia, and Poland prepared their security cadres in the Soviet Union right up to 1989).[30] Reduced cooperation does not mean,

13

however, that the Soviet Union was ignorant of what the Romanians were up to: when the Securitate installed its computerized database in 1971, using a state-of-the-art IBM computer (obtained through barter, to reduce the drain on hard currency), the installers were East German Stasi engineers. Given the close collaboration between the Stasi and the KGB, it is not unlikely that the new Romanian system was made vulnerable to Soviet penetration.[31]

Interorganizational Relations and Changes over Time

Importantly for what I will argue in chapter 2, the Securitate existed in a constantly shifting interorganizational ecology. In the mid-1950s, as part of revisions following Stalin's death, it got rid of 70 percent of its informers and numerous agents considered to be "fascists," leaving many of its actions of the late 1950s inadequately supported.[32] At the same time, the organization was in a constant struggle with the Romanian Communist Party, which strove to bring it under firmer control so as to reduce communication of the Party's activities to the KGB through Securitate channels. In 1954 and 1957, for instance, the Romanian Politburo began limiting what the Securitate could do with respect to Party members, upon whom it had spied without constraint until then. This included ruling that Party First Secretaries in the regions and Party Secretaries in the districts should know who the Securitate agents were within their jurisdictions, and that the Party must approve any use of Party members as Securitate informers.[33] The limitations increased the Party's control over the Securitate, further reinforced after Soviet troops were withdrawn from Romania in 1958.[34] After Nicolae Ceaușescu became General Secretary in 1965, the Securitate's influence was further reduced because its head, Alexandru Drăghici, had been Ceaușescu's main rival for the leadership.[35] When Drăghici was excluded from both the Party and his job, the competitive relations between the Party and Securitate were decisively resolved in the Party's favor, and the interorganizational environment acquired greater stability.

The provisional equilibrium achieved by 1970 applied chiefly to relations among the Soviets, the Romanian Party, and the Securitate. Relations *within* the Romanian intelligence apparatus, however, were far from stable. As is true in many secret services around the world,[36] frictions continually erupted between the internal and external branches and among segments of each of them, as well as between the Securitate and army-based intelligence units.[37] In addition,

15

the organization's place within the government continued to change, as it was now subordinated to the
Interior Ministry, now part of a free-standing Council of State Security, now part of the Interior Ministry again. The most significant conflicts involved the
Foreign Intelligence Service (Department of External
Information, or DIE, the Romanian CIA), whose officers considered themselves superior to those of other branches, which they were moving to bring under
DIE aegis.[38] The defection of the DIE deputy head,
General Ion Mihai Pacepa, to the US in 1978 produced havoc within the Securitate, which Ceaușescu
then personally rebuilt and strengthened, bringing it
more firmly under his direct control and elevating it
to the rank of ministry.[39]

Ceaușescu's rise to power brought a number of
other changes, including a change in the Securitate's
mandate, "from 'destroying the class enemy' to 'preventing infractions against state security' and 'defending fundamental national values.'"[40] Recruitment
policies sought to attract younger and better educated people by offering very large salaries and possibilities for travel. In the early 1970s psychological testing
began, which revealed that "half of those in the operative departments did not have the qualities necessary
for an intelligence officer," so they were transferred
to nonoperative or bureaucratic divisions or to the re-

serves.[41] By 1973, 100 percent of the leading Securitate cadres had been replaced through increased educational requirements. In 1974, Ceauşescu launched a new mission for the Securitate: the "war of the entire people,"[42] which would have important consequences for the recruitment of informers, as I will discuss in chapter 3. This was part of a growing effort to mobilize the wider population and included a shift (already evident in the 1960s) away from violent action toward more discreet forms of surveillance and persuasion. In the late socialist period, the Securitate increasingly became a pedagogical or didactic rather than a punitive institution.[43]

This broadened recruitment of the populace did not mean, however, a dwindling reliance on other surveillance methods: on the contrary. In the 1970s a world-wide expansion of new surveillance technologies affected Romania as well as other bloc countries. In East Germany, for example, Macrakis reports that in 1972, there was a 291 percent increase in requests for surveillance technology for use against people trying to flee and in 1974 a six-fold increase with respect to eavesdropping equipment.[44] Vatulescu discusses the impact of new technologies for Romania, as well, commenting on the more impersonal tone. She finds changes in the character of the file kept, for example, on Orthodox priest and dissident writer Nicolae

Steinhardt as of 1972, when they installed bugging devices in his house.[45] Thus, these technologies transformed the data base on which the Securitate would now rely and the interpretations they could develop.

During the 1980s, Romania's economic performance worsened, and at the same time, Soviet *perestroika* increased Ceaușescu's fear that Mikhail Gorbachev intended to displace him. These developments had important consequences for the Securitate. Relations with neighboring Hungary (a Gorbachev ally) worsened: the more Hungary opened to the West and relaxed surveillance, the more anxious the Securitate became about possible agitation among Romania's Hungarian minority and the tighter grew its control over the populace, giving it more work to do. The leadership's anxiety over the consequences of declining standards of living aggravated this repression, further widening the gap between the two neighboring countries. Economic difficulties caused Ceaușescu to create a special department within the Securitate to conduct hard-currency business deals that might help to keep Romania's economy afloat. But the result was to aggravate organizational instability further, for the vital role of hard currency in paying off the foreign debt gave the officers of that unit a position of special privilege.[46] This same decade also saw an intensification of the idea that Securitate officers were "Party activists in a special domain," which—joined with Ceaușescu's idea that Party activists are "revolutionaries by profession"—made officers into "professional revolutionaries in a special domain." That completed their debasement from a well trained intelligence force to propagandists and bodyguards for the dictator.[47] The defection of some Securitate factions in December 1989 sealed his fate and ensured that at least some parts of the organization would survive the "revolution" intact. They morphed into the Romanian Information Service (SRI), and their members entered one or another of the several intelligence organizations set up by post-1989 governments.

Securitate, Power, and Affect

These details about its formation and organizational ecology are not, however, a sufficient answer to the question "What Was the Securitate?" To flesh it out further, I invoke the work of Hungarian sociologists Ágnes Horváth and Árpád Szakolczai in *The Dissolution of Communist Power*. Following previous scholars of Bolshevik-type regimes such as Kenneth Jowitt,[48] they emphasize the regimes' essentially mobilizational character and the attempt to colonize routine elements of behavior, penetrating daily life more fully than any

19

modern regime hitherto. Such regimes, these authors suggest, therefore resemble the early modern police, whose "area of competence included everything related to the common activities of individuals, their health, wealth and happiness.... The goal of the police was not restricted to the formulation of the space where the co-harmonisation of state and individual concerns became possible; it was extended to the moulding of individuals as well."[49] Other commonalities include "a concern with all sorts of activities, and in minute detail" and "the direct, overriding importance of the promotion of the public good" as justification for police activities.[50] They conclude, "Perhaps the most important common characteristic of the early modern 'police' and the bolshevik-type state-party is the preoccupation with order, the need to establish and maintain order at any price."[51]

Although other scholars have made comparable observations, they have not rooted those, as do Horváth and Szakolczai, in the concept of power they believe underlay Soviet rule: a concept that resurrected the Greek notion of "power as *arkhé*, as initiative, as opposed to the idea that power is simply rule or position. The consequence was that bolshevism tried to influence and supervise all decisions, all movements, all initiatives. ... It tried at once to destroy and then to replace, stimulate and instigate all activities."[52] Compare the wording of Romanian scholar Florian Banu, who writes that what distinguished the Securitate from Romania's previous informational regimes was "[a] boundless ambition, ideologically motivated, to know EVERYTHING, to control EVERYTHING and to repress EVERY anticommunist gesture, idea, or attitude."[53] These phrasings are reminiscent, as well, of Jan Gross's concept of communism's "spoiler state," which destroys all possible foci of initiative outside itself,[54] and of Caroline Humphrey's conclusion that "[t]he cultural concepts of the 'domain' (*khoziaistvo*) and the state (*gosudarstvo*) encode in themselves from the beginning the reification of political entities in which a central personification of power creates order."[55]

If power in this context is culturally understood as initiative and the creation of order, then crucial to its exercise is discovering and eliminating anything that might block it, that might infringe upon initiative and prevent order. The secret police was the vital organ—the biological imagery comes from the language of the regimes themselves—assigned to that task. It was preeminently an organ of vigilance, discovering sources of disorder and neutralizing them. Its job was to distinguish friend from enemy—a preoccupation evident as early as Lenin's instructing Felix Dzerzhinsky, in December 1917, to draft a decree "'on the struggle with

21

counter-revolutionary saboteurs'"; the result was the formation of the Cheka, the first of many Soviet security services.[56] Julie Fedor writes, "[T]he enemy provided the chekist's whole *raison d'être*. Without the existence of the enemy, the chekist is unthinkable, and unjustifiable."[57] The Securitate was similar. Tăbăcaru contrasts it with the army: the army fights on an *open* front against a *known* enemy in *specific campaigns*, the Securitate fights on a *closed* front against an *un*known enemy, *continually*.[58] Both specialize in routing an enemy, and this requires acts of classification to distinguish enemies from friends. The Securitate assumed that enemies were everywhere; it had a fundamentally agonistic world view and employed a language of military metaphors. For example, officers saw the organization as engaged in "battle" to cleanse Romanian society of its enemies—which included foreign "spies" like myself—, and they called the people they were following "targets" (*obiectivi*), understood in the military sense.

There are many ways to organize the relation between enemy and friend, rooted in different ways of understanding threat and danger. Buck-Morss succinctly captures two contrasting political imaginaries through which west European and Bolshevik states organized the relation of friend and enemy: the west European one of mutually exclusive, potentially hostile nation-states, and the Bolshevik one of irreconcilably antagonistic warring classes.[59] For Soviet-type systems, that initial source of danger, the class enemy, was later expanded into national enemies, foreign spies, irredentists, and so forth. The work of the secret police concerned just such classification: how to categorize people, and what evidence to use for doing so. They did not invent the categorizations but took their cue from the Party leadership, initially the *Soviet* Party leadership.[60] Implementing the distinctions, however, was their job. In their world view, the existence of enemies was implicit, inscribed in the very concept of power as initiative. They would often *produce* such enemies in the process of "uncovering" them, for once such a role was created to justify an institution's existence, people would be found to fill it.

All countries have intelligence services concerned with spying and the maintenance of internal order, and they share a number of practices regardless of so-cio-political system. They also share real dilemmas in balancing the important requirements of national security with respect for citizens' rights (a balance problematically struck, for example, in US policy toward terrorism suspects after September 11, 2001). Nonetheless, not all states accord so unbridled a mandate to their intelligence services as did Bolshevik-type regimes. Their origins in an illegal movement persecuted by the tsarist police strengthened their obsession

23

both with secrecy and with ferreting out information that might reveal conspiracies. What Banu calls the "secretomania" of the Romanian regime emerged directly from Soviet imagery of the Party as a "beseiged castle" facing enemies both within and without.[61] These origins, combined with the magnitude of the mobilizational and transformative task the regimes faced, contributed to one of the most signal features of their security services: the use of fear.

In every social system, as part of the subjectivities proper to them, there develop characteristic organizations of affect, or sentiment—characteristic ideas about what kinds of people have what kinds of feelings ("emotional" women vs. "stoical" men), for instance, or patterns of desire cultivated through market forces. Numerous scholars, such as Lynn Hunt (for revolutionary France), Mabel Berezin (for fascist Italy), and Neringa Klumbyte (for Soviet Lithuania), have explored the means by which this occurs.[62] Although the extent to which specifically *state* organs strive to manipulate or play upon affect differs from case to case and across time, literature on what Raymond Williams famously called "structures of feeling" strongly suggests that the cultivation of affect is an important part of state-making.[63] A particularly significant affect is fear. Corey Robin, in his book *Fear: The History of a Political Idea*, examines the history of fear in state-making, showing that some political philosophers, such as Thomas Hobbes, made fear *pre*-political, the basis for creating the state as a provider of security.[64] But fear often results from the actions of state agents themselves. In the US, government action in the "Red Scare" of the 1950s as well as the war on terror after September 11, 2001, explicitly heightened citizens' anxiety even while claiming to protect them. Commenting on the permanent state of fear, suspicion, and anxiety the Securitate created, historian Cristian Troncotă writes: "In a word, the Security forces were the principal factor that created *in*security."[65]

In the division of labor among segments of rule in Soviet-type socialism (Party, police, state apparatus, and so on), the job of creating fear as a pervasive subject disposition went primarily to the NKVD/KGB and its offshoots in Eastern Europe, including the Stasi and the Securitate. As Anisescu puts it, "These two instances of communist state power in Romania, Party and Securitate, held complementary functions— social control and forming consciousness—using toward these ends manipulation through indoctrination, terror and the 'redistribution of fear,' 'through creating a climate of virtual threat.'"[66] A chief task of the Party was to create joy, élan, confidence that "things are getting better and better," with an eye to transforming consciousness. The police, by contrast,

25

trafficked in dread. In all of the socialist countries, fear was integrated into state-making variably across time and space. Over time, fear of the "black car" and the midnight knock on the door gave way to a more diffuse fear of the subtle reprisals the Securitate might take if one refused to cooperate with them, along with fear of being a possible target of informers. On the whole, the worst fear-generating excesses ended in the Soviet Union with Stalin's death and in Eastern Europe by the mid to late 1960s, though the timing varied for different countries. But one could also argue, as I will suggest in chapter 3, that although the actions of the Securitate became less overtly violent, fear became more intimately lodged in people through the manner in which the police colonized social relationships and generated collusion, blurring the line between perpetrators and others and sowing mistrust at the heart of social relations.

The idea had been to contain enemies, by teaching the population to fear them; but ultimately it was the Securitate they came to fear. Although fear of the enemy would ideally produce solidarity against him and support for the communists, the means through which fear was aroused tended, rather, to individualize and divide. Essential to these effects was its invisibility—as Glaeser writes of the Stasi, "precisely because it was hiding, it was imagined to be everywhere."[67] In this sense, we could contrast the emotion-generating practices Berezin discusses for fascist Italy or Foucault for early modern France[68]—emphasizing the fearsome public spectacle—with the practices of the rarely seen communist secret services. I will return to this point in chapter 2. Also essential to the fear the Securitate generated was its gendering, for the great majority of security police were male, and this infused the organization's work with gendered expectations of force, prepotency, and violence.

The irony in the Securitate's manipulation of fear was that it affected even the police and Party members themselves, contributing to the obsession with control. As Anisescu puts it, "Behind these needs to control everything lay a paralyzing sense of fear, generated by the uncontrollable, by the fact that 'something still exists in the souls, the thoughts, and the life of people that is slipping through their fingers, that subtracts itself from control, that has not yet been brought under control.'"[69] Oprea states that Securitate officers experienced "fear of the discretionary power of their own apparatus, which they perceived at close quarters with a healthy appreciation for its destructiveness."[70] A Party member who had worked in the state administration described to me his persistent terror (resulting in a nervous breakdown) that someone would discover his "unhealthy social origin" and take away his job, or worse. Another acquaintance who once taught in the Securitate academy put it, simply: "*We* were afraid too. Everyone was watching everyone." The reason: from the Party's point of view, the greatest danger of all could come from its own cadres, those who might disagree with decisions, promote an alternative vision, or serve the accumulation of power and resources in alternative centers.[71] The enemies the Securitate pursued were not first and foremost among the population at large but among the political elite.

To see the Securitate as inhabiting a space defined by danger, enemies, and fear is to position it in the most elemental area in politics. Such a view will discomfit readers who see the secret police (indeed, the entire communist system) as inhabiting, rather, the space of evil. I believe my view enables ethnography better, by facilitating a suspension of Cold War stereotypes and helping us to treat the Securitate as an entity with its own unfolding historicity. This is not to deny, however, that the space of fear and danger might attract people with a propensity for brutality or evil who would take pleasure in terrorizing others, nor is it to render that space structurally innocent. Their place in the architecture of a totalizing system whose order they served to maintain gave their actions disproportionate weight.

* * *

In the three essays to follow, I employ a variety of theoretical lenses to approach the Securitate and its files ethnographically. The first chapter provides an overview of the Securitate archive and a description of some of the practices it reveals. These include a fundamental practice of secret police work that appears throughout the book: what I call "conspirativity," or compartmentalization, which was designed to preserve secrecy of operations. In this chapter I discuss three questions: what is the Securitate archive, how can we characterize its files, and what do those files do? For that last question I will write about both their creation of persons and their material effects in the bureaucracy, borrowing from Ian Hacking's notion of "making up people" and from a combination of semiotic anthropology and actor-network theory. In the second chapter I explore the suggestion, proposed by Hannah Arendt and others, that the secret police were a form of secret society. Using some ideas from the anthropological literature on that subject, I will explore what secrecy meant for the Securitate, emphasizing the effects of conspirativity and the consequences of secrecy for socialism's legitimation. In the third chapter I take my cue from Foucault to ask about the knowledge practices revealed in the Securitate files—practices many of which are no doubt shared with other intelligence services, not to mention social groups of other kinds. I will focus particularly on the officers' use of informers and their attention to networks. I end the book with some observations about the relevance of work on the Securitate for the rapidly developing "security state" of our neoliberal present.

Chapter 1

An Archive and Its Fictions

> In the socialist bloc, people and things exist only through their files. All our existence is in the hands of him who possesses files and is constituted by him who constructs them. Real people are but the reflection of their files.
>
> — Belu Zilber [1]

As I noted in the Introduction, after the fall of communism many East European countries created lustration procedures to scrutinize candidates for public office. These procedures, where they were instituted, relied heavily (even if very problematically) on the files of the secret police. Romania, however, was slow to embark on lustration. Whereas Czechoslovakia and Germany were lustrating by 1990-91, in Romania it was only in 1999 that legislation provided access to secret police files and a procedure for vetting public officials, and the process suffered numerous reversals. An organization, the National Council for the Study of the Securitate Archives, known by its Romanian acronym CNSAS, was founded in 2000 to administer the archive and mediate public access to the files, which it took over from the various agencies (largely successor organizations to the Securitate) that had overseen them for the eleven years following Ceaușescu's overthrow.[2]

The procedures for taking over the archive were protracted and fraught, as the various agencies transferred their segments only piecemeal and in small numbers until after the elections of 2004, which brought a new political coalition to power. In 2005 over one million files were turned over, with more following thereafter, although the total corpus of the Securitate files is even now not fully under CNSAS control. Inadequate space and technology for managing the material, not to mention purposeful "loss" of files, further hampered its transfer. As of 2013 the CNSAS archive consists of over 1,800,000 paper files in 2,300,000 volumes and a variety of other media; about 70 percent of the total archive is in paper files, 25 percent in microfilms, and 5 percent in audio and video material.[3] As for lustration itself, in 2006 the first of several lustration laws was passed and then rejected as unconstitutional, a sequence repeated several times thereafter. Despite these ups and downs of the lustration law, the CNSAS has continued to make files available to many persons who request them—including citizens of NATO countries like myself, who are permitted access to their files.[4]

The Securitate Archive and Its Files

The archive is divided into multiple fonds, the principal ones being surveillance files of targets (the term I will use for people under surveillance); files of people who collaborated with the Securitate in one form or another; documentary files on particular problems such as religion, foreign researchers, art, and so forth; files from the Foreign Intelligence Service (DIE, renamed SIE); internal administrative documents and the personnel files of Securitate employees; and confiscated manuscripts. The CNSAS archive's total volume is approximately twenty-four kilometers[5]—surprisingly small, when one considers that the Polish SB files occupy about eighty kilometers and the Stasi files well over one hundred kilometers, for a smaller population.[6] At least part of the reason for the differences is that a sizable portion of the original Securitate documents was destroyed, both accidentally and intentionally[7]—either through normal administrative procedures during the communist period[8] or through events relating to the 1989 revolution, when buildings containing files caught fire and truckloads of documents were found burned and partially buried outside Bucharest.[9] More generally, however, it is impossible to say how large the archive was or is. At the time of the revolution it existed in various county offices around the country, sometimes with copies in the central archive in Bucharest but without precise collation. For someone like me to request a file could involve bringing volumes of papers not only from the depository on the city's outskirts to the CNSAS building in Bucharest but also from several different county headquarters as well. Each such request entailed that someone look through the material and withhold anything considered to be critical to national security; what was then transferred to CNSAS would thus be only a partial file. The endless politicking around lustration as well as other peculiarities of the process of file transfer mean that the archive now under CNSAS control—what is usually meant by the term "Securitate archive"—is a heavily politicized remnant, the result of several political churnings of the original.[10]

Twenty-four or so kilometers is still a large archive. What more can we say about it? Romanian researcher Florin Poenaru offers several observations, drawing upon Michel-Rolph Trouillot's work *Silencing the Past*, which sees an archive as the sum not only of recorded documents but of silences.[11] One peculiarity of the Securitate archive, suggests Poenaru, is that it has at least *two* levels of "silences": the one Trouillot describes, having to do with the ontological gap between a historical event and its recording, which leaves room for selective retention and processes of power, and a second level relating to the fact that "the Securitate archive was created by and against the silence of the population being monitored. As it were, the role of the Securitate archive was to record everything that was being kept silent by the population. ... The task of the historian, in this case, might not necessarily be that of navigating and making sense of the silences inherent in the archives [as Trouillot would have it], or to put it differently, to historicize its gaps and selections, but to understand and deal with its loquacity, not with its lack but with its excess, not with what is missing but with what is already present there."[12] Poenaru's reference to the archive's "loquacity" reminds one of Stephen Kotkin's observation, following upon Lefort's comments about the loquaciousness of the Stalinist state: "Stalinism could not stop speaking about itself. ... The advent of Stalinism brought one of the greatest proliferations of documents the world has ever seen."[13] It is to that habit that we owe the existence of this extensive archive.

Poenaru goes on to note another difference between a regular archive and the Securitate's. Unlike a standard archive, which includes some people and obscures the voices, experiences and even existence of others (women, black people in the triumphal histories of colonialism, and so forth), who therefore have

35

to find ways of resisting their erasure, the Securitate archive reverses the situation: "people included in it have always felt the need to justify themselves, to give an account of this inclusion (either as 'perpetrators,' or as 'victims'), or to erase their inclusion, to make it disappear."[14] In short, rather than resisting their exclusion, most people who find themselves in this archive would much rather not be there.

A final observation about the form of the archive concerns how the authority of its contents is expressed. Former Party member and political prisoner Belu Zilber writes,

> Handwriting doesn't inspire too much confidence in the ordinary reader, even if it carries an illustrious signature. The same handwritten item, when typed, gains clarity and authority... Files contain almost entirely sheets written on a typewriter. Their authority proceeds from this... The process that led to the consolidation of state formations through the appearance of the printing press repeated itself at the culmination of the Stalinist state through the appearance of the typewriter. Only thanks to Remington's invention could we arrive at the principle: a person and a file having the authority of the state. It is not by chance that until recently, in Russia only state offices had typewriters.[15]

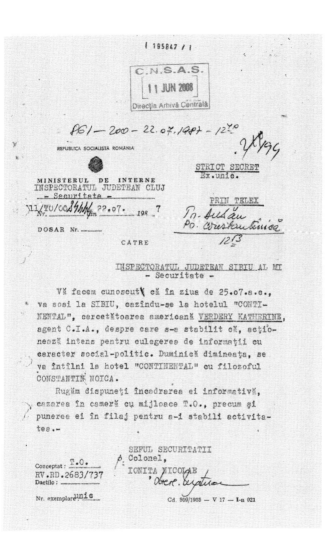

P6/ — 200 - 22.07.1987 - 12⁰⁰

REPUBLICA SOCIALISTĂ ROMÂNIA

STRICT SECRET
Ex.unic.

MINISTERUL DE INTERNE
INSPECTORATUL JUDEȚEAN CLUJ
— Securitate —

Nr. 11/TO/00........ din ??.07. 198 7

PRIN TELEX

DOSAR Nr. ....

CATRE

INSPECTORATUL JUDEȚEAN SIBIU AL MI
— Securitate —

Vă facem cunoscut că în ziua de 25.07.a.c., va sosi la SIBIU, cazîndu-se la hotelul "CONTINENTAL", cercetătoarea americană VERDERY KATHERINE, agent C.I.A., despre care s-a stabilit că, acționează intens pentru culegerea de informații cu caracter social-politic. Duminică dimineața, se va întîlni la hotel "CONTINENTAL" cu filozoful CONSTANTIN NOICA.

Rugăm dispuneți încadrarea ei informativă, cazarea în cameră cu mijloace T.O., precum și punerea ei în filaj pentru a-i stabili activitatea.—

SEFUL SECURITATII
Colonel,
IONIȚA NICOLAE

Conceptat: T.O.
RV.RD.2683/737
Dactilo: ....

Nr. exemplare unic

Cd. 509/1985 — V 17 — I-n 021

Figure 1.1. Normal font for lower-level documents

37

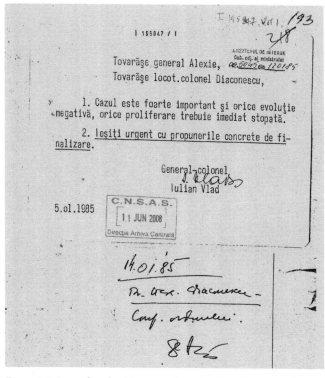

Figure 1.2. Large font for documents from top Securitate generals

In Securitate files, an officer's handwritten notes are generally replaced (or doubled) with typed versions, especially after the 1950s. Handwriting persists, of course, in the marginal notes of people to whom a file circulates, and sometimes in the notes of someone reporting on a telephone conversation. Informers' reports often remain in the informer's hand, however, preserving traces of the pedagogical process by which they were generated (the officer and the informer together working out what should go in the report, as one of my own informers described it to me).[16] But informers and telephone operators are the lowliest of actors in this universe; anyone of importance will have his text typed. Indeed, in my own file and some others I have seen, the importance of the sender appears in the font: normal case reports are in a font resembling Times Roman 12 point, whereas documents coming from the top generals are in one resembling Tahoma 16 point (see Figures 1.1 and 1.2).[17]

Unlike many administrative archives, such as the one described in Matthew Hull's fascinating *Government by Paper* about Pakistan's bureaucracy,[18] this one does not constitute primarily a record of administrative actions requested and taken but a site at which knowledge about "reality" was concentrated through collecting endless amounts of information. This leads toward seeing the archive as a kind of ethnographic data base—not primarily concerning the lives of the people under surveillance but concerning the inner workings of this branch of the Party-state. Literary scholar Cristina Vatulescu makes a similar point: "Sometimes wildly skewed records of historical fact, the files are at the same time priceless representations of the values, apprehensions, and fantasies entertained by the secret police. While a personal file can mislead about the particulars of a victim's fate, its close reading can be abundantly revealing about what the secret police understood by evidence, record, writing, human nature, and criminality."[19] In the case of my own surveillance file, my long-term goal is to treat its 2,780 pages as if they were someone's fieldnotes, attempting to reconstruct from them the world view and practices of the officers and informers who produced them. What operation of power do these files reveal? What regime of truth or knowledge do they assume and attempt to serve, and how is it connected with power? What sort of knowledge-production enterprise do we see in them? How can we characterize what they are after? What common practices emerge from this body of evidence, and what categories and discursive frames? How do they define their object? What does the language of the files tell us about their makers' epistemology?

Conspirativity

Although I will not seek to answer these questions now through my file, let me briefly use it to illustrate the archive's potential for doing so. For example: my overall impression from reading my file—an opinion shared by others who have read theirs—is of an extraordinary expenditure of time, money, and effort.[20] The Securitate's work is very labor-intensive. Officers not only photograph or copy my field notes: they translate them into Romanian in painstaking error-filled drafts, then have those typed. Someone then reads the notes and underlines certain passages (occasionally with a gratifying 'Yes!' or other commentary indicating that I am right). Endless hours are devoted to translating correspondence and transcribing recorded conversations that sometimes lasted an entire evening. Agents charged with following me spend 14-, 16-, 18-hour days, much of the time waiting for me to leave one building and go into another.[21] Documents, accompanied by cover letters and marginal notations, are circulated up and back down the reporting hierarchy, where they are read and notated. Case officers meet with informers, then have to write their reports and (generally) have those typed. Having determined that my contact with villagers who were commuting to work in an armaments factory is a problem, they draw up a list of all people living in every nearby settlement who work there, so they can contact these people and warn them against me, as well as seeking to recruit informers among them. The list gives not only the people's names but those of their parents, their places and dates of birth, and the specifics of their occupations (imagine how much time it took to get that for some 138 people); notations indicate those who already serve as informers.[22]

This was very time-consuming work; clearly I occupied enormous amounts of Securitate man-hours.[23] Moreover, the file betrays a remarkable duplication of effort. Similar texts provide similar information from different officers; wording is copied from one text to another and retyped. Sometimes it seems one department has no idea what others already know; they recreate the same discovery. As ex-informer Nicolae Corbeanu puts it in his memoir, "Recollections of a coward": "I always had the impression that in the Securitate, at least at the local level, the left hand didn't much know what the right hand was doing."[24]

What can we make of all this seemingly wasteful duplication of effort? Was it just good sleuthing—data that are replicated are more credible? Does it betray a pedagogical practice: the point was not (just) to get specific information about a person but to train many people in a process of producing it, through the repetition and circulation of a limited set of categories and techniques? Perhaps the point was not to produce information efficiently at all but rather to demonstrate that the officers were working hard; therefore the idea of "wasteful effort" makes no sense. In a system that rewarded people according to the fulfillment of production plans (which included plans for recruiting informers), proof of completing planned activity was indeed very important.[25] But I think the most important cause of this duplicative effort is to be found in practices aimed both at specialization and at maintaining the secrecy of Securitate personnel—practices of what they called *conspirativitate*, which I will translate as "conspirativity," an aspect of the compartmentalization of intelligence work that is common to all secret services.

Securitate actions were segmented into different branches—following people ("Service F"), censoring correspondence ("Service S"), intercepting telephone conversations ("Service T"), disinformation ("Service D"), and so on—as well as into different directorates specializing in internal information (Directorate I,) counterespionage (Directorate III), military counterespionage (IV), and so forth. Each of these had its corps of agents, divided by county and district. The principle of conspirativity dictated that agents from one branch not deal directly with agents from another, to reduce the possibility that someone's identity would be discovered.[26] According to Oprea, this kind of compartmentalization was a basic principle of the Securitate's work. It aimed to increase the secrecy surrounding its activity, known in its entirety only by the top leaders and those of the Interior Ministry.

He writes, "Officers of one department could get data or information from another only by going through their chiefs. Any divulging of their own activity and its results to colleagues from other departments was drastically sanctioned, on the basis of violating conspirativity and the principle of 'compartmentalization of the work of the Securitate.' The levels of access to information concerning the activities of the Securitate were clearly delimited."[27]

Conspirativity appears in multiple forms. One example comes from the Hungarian documentary film "Az Ügynök Élete" (The Life of an Agent), made from a top-secret collection of training films for secret police, which notes that after the projectionist started a film for the trainees, he had to leave the room in the interests of conspirativity.[28] Figure 1.3 shows another example from a case officer's report. Whoever typed the report from the officer's notes was not given the name of the person about whom the report was written; she typed blank lines, onto which the officer would later fill in the names by hand, so the typist would not be able to associate the officer with a particular target. A third example comes from the instructions for relations between informers and their minders: If an informant on the way to meet his officer sees him on the street, he must cross the street and pretend he does not know him.[29]

- 2 -

- să se revadă materialele obţinute despre *VERDERY KATHERINE* în perioada 1973/1974 cu ocazia vizitei anterioare ce a efectuat-o în jud. Hunedoara, cînd au fost obţinute unele date că cea în cauză ar manifesta interes pentru culegerea de informaţii cu caracter militar.

- în perioada cît *VERDERY KATHERINE* se va afla din nou pe raza judeţului Hunedoara, să se întreprindă măsuri informativ-operative complexe pentru a se stabili dacă are sau nu preocupări de natură informativă;

- în cadrul măsurilor ce vor fi întreprinse să se stabilească faptul dacă cea în cauză îşi extinde cercetările şi asupra altor date care nu au legătură cu tema pentru care a primit aprobare, în scopul de a se putea interveni din timp să i se limiteze accestul;

- să se comunice în timp util toate deplasările lui *VERDERY KATHERINE* în alte localităţi din afara judeţului Hunedoara, atît la Direcţia a III-a, cît şi la organele de securitate judeţene interesate, pentru a se continua măsurile de supraveghere a celei în cauză.

Datele obţinute din urmărirea activităţii lui *VERDERY KATHERINE*, rugăm să ne fie comunicate periodic.

LOCŢIITOR ȘEF DIRECŢIE,
Colonel,
Ionescu, Vergiliu

C.N.S.A.S.
2 3 JUL 2008
DIRECŢIA ARHIVĂ CENTRALĂ

MD/PS/ex.unic.
RD 2624/16.11.979

Figure 1.3. Conspirativity: Report with blank lines, later filled in

45

Conspirativity had two aspects, relating to inside and outside the organization: 1) Compartmentalization of work in the unit in such a way that each person knows only as much as needed, and each busies himself with his own cases and problems—about which no one should know except those invested with this right; 2) Preserving the secret of one's work outside the unit, of actions taken, of the means used.[30] The first of these referred to hiding the work of the apparatus from itself by disguising the work of officers from each other, the second to hiding the work of informers, whose identities (like those of the targets being followed) were disguised with pseudonyms. A document containing instructions for operative surveillance gives some examples:

> [People doing this work] wear only civil clothing and are registered at their domicile as workers in one or another institution/firm, carrying special documents to this effect... Under-cover workers are not allowed to live in houses of Interior Ministry organs or come into contact with uncovered Securitate workers, to be photographed in groups, to participate in political manifestations of Securitate workers, or to be used in official actions of Securitate organs... Visiting the Securitate headquarters or workplaces by under-cover workers is permitted only in exceptional cases and each case must be approved by the lead-

ership of that organ. … They must preserve strict conspirativity. [If it is breached, the consequences include] transferring the worker to another city or his removal from the Securitate. Units of the apparatus of operative surveillance are located in special under-cover headquarters, each with its own cover. … It is categorically forbidden for uncovered operative workers to visit the under-cover headquarters in their Securitate uniforms… It is not permitted… to have phone conversations from which it might be concluded that the telephone belongs to the Securitate, nor to communicate to any person, including Securitate workers having no connection with the activity of operative surveillance, the addresses of the under-cover headquarters.[31]

The true identity of officers of the most highly secretized units was known only by their hierarchical superiors and the head of the central personnel division. After the defection of General Pacepa, a special unit 0544 was formed that was completely under-cover; its officers were not known to other Securitate officers, and even the head of it did not participate in its meetings for analysis.[32]

Here is a specific example of how problems of conspirativity might appear in a person's file (see Figure 1.4). You are looking at a Securitate officer, who is facing me in 1988 in the one episode during my more than three years in Romania when I knowingly stood face to face with a *Securist* (I recall him as more menacing in person). The officer stands in front of an apartment building in which I was to meet an important Romanian writer; he has just asked me for my papers and informed me that if this visit is not part of my officially approved research program, I do not have permission to enter the building. In his handwriting on these photos is the note, "Moment of warning 'VERA'" (one of my code names).

When I showed this photo to two researchers at CNSAS, both were astonished: an officer should *never* appear in a photo with his target, not even in a secret file. It is a breach of conspirativity. One of these two researchers speculated that my interlocutor's superior officer had made the mistake of not properly directing my shadow (the person following me), but of course that would have revealed the officer to my shadow, breaching conspirativity: the shadower should not know who my case officer was. Instead, the officer should have remained inside the building, *invisible* to my shadow, and then accosted me when I entered, thereby avoiding the camera. By walking out, he had uncovered (*deconspirat*) himself. In any case, the photo shows that whoever was in charge had not done what was necessary to preserving the officer's anonym-

Figure 1.4. Failure of conspirativity: a Securitate officer accosts "VERA" and has his picture taken

ity. Particularly interesting, however, is the possibility, suggested by the handwriting on the note, that the officer himself had placed the photograph in my file. My second CNSAS interlocutor attributed that possibilty to "an excess of zeal: he wanted his superiors to know he had carried out his mission of giving you a warning." Whatever the interpretation, having his photo and handwriting samples means I now know who accosted me.

As I will discuss further in chapter 2, the demands of conspirativity vastly complicated the Securitate's work, contributing to its inefficiencies and duplication of effort as well as to a considerable amount of organizational incoherence. For example, according to Troncotă, various units and compartments involved in counterinformation across the territory had their own systems of evidence and archives. Therefore, he suggests, if the Securitate was a hyper-centralized institution, that was not true in the domain of the archives, where decentralization reigned owing to the principles of compartmentalization and secrecy.[33] The workings of conspirativity as a practice, combined with my earlier comments about factionalism within the organization and its complex relations with other branches of government, invites us to see the Securitate not as a monolith with a single overriding intention—the opinion of most Romanian citizens—but as a multicentric organization fragmented among many parts.

Properties of the Files

The segmentation of work practices is amply evident in the files themselves. My own consists of informers reports, letters that have been copied and often translated, often-lengthy transcripts of telephone conversations or conversations secretly recorded in one or another public place (sometimes these are verbatim, sometimes just summaries), photographs—of me, of people I am with, of my research notes—, painstaking translations of these notes, detailed logs of the officers who followed me on my daily rounds, action plans for dealing with me, lengthy reports by officers synthesizing the situation revealed by all this, and the marginal notes of one or more superior officers who read them. In a word, a Securitate file is a heteroglossic body of documents, nearly all of it obtained in secret, produced by a variety of people using a range of linguistic conventions. It is polyphonic as well, not only because so many different services contribute to it but because of the multiple notations in the margins by people who have read any given document; thus, any one page can contain the voices of several readers.

Let me dwell for a moment on the file's heteroglossia, in connection with Bakhtin's idea of heteroglossia in the novel.[34] This is not a completely nonsensical move, for the files are replete with fantasy and invented characters, though not from conscious authorial intent. For Bakhtin, heteroglossia—the coexistence of multiple speech varieties or voices within a single text, utterance, or national language, reflecting multiple points of view—was the defining characteristic of the novel and the source of its power. That power, in turn, was used to call into question authoritative discourse, a form that demands unconditional acceptance by the hearer and permits no alternative

51

interpretation. The "officialese" of Communist Party enunciations is a typical instance of authoritative discourse. Securitate files contain multiple voices and viewpoints—the voice of the target, of the case officers and other operative workers, of superior officers in the hierarchy, of the informers (who sometimes parrot the voice of the Party as they understand it), and so on. But unlike a novel, the work of the file is to *decontextualize* those other voices and subject them to a single dominant interpretation, by attributing meanings to the target as viewed through the lenses of the various workers and by reinterpreting the target's own utterances and acts. If in Bakhtin's view the novel's effectiveness comes from the coexistence of, and conflict among, different types of utterance, with authors' intentions expressed only indirectly through the way they yoke different voices, then the effectiveness of the file in its context lies in its goal of reducing the variety of meanings in the multiple voices it contains so as to leave only one interpretation: the target's identification as an enemy.

The organization of a surveillance file is not chronological but activity-based. As described by Troncotă,[35] the first item is not the reports that caused a person to be followed but a case officer's proposal to set up a surveillance file; after it come informational reports generally dated prior to that proposal and justifying it (the elapsed time indicates the period necessary to verify the information in them). Then comes the action plan (*plan de măsuri*), laying out the measures to be taken so as to verify the danger the target posed, and after that the periodic reports of the case officer and his superiors presenting conclusions to date and further measures to be taken.[36] A given file would usually group all these action plans together, likewise the analytic reports, even if they were separated in time by several months. After this group of documents came others resulting from the action plan, in chronological order but grouped by the service that produced them: all informers' notes together, all logs of shadowing the suspect, all censored correspondence, all overheard conversations, and so on. As a result, Troncotă notes, research into a file is very cumbersome since one cannot follow the thread of an action from beginning to end; the system was apparently useful, however, for the operative who wanted to work with it and who wanted not to read the entire file but merely to look for a specific kind of information (informer's reports, correspondence, and so on), which he would find all together. The final page in the file would be a proposal to close the surveillance action, giving the reason for opening it, the measures taken, and the reason for closing it, along with the approval of superior officers. After this, the file went to the archivists, who would read the entire thing, remove extraneous items, perhaps underline important passages, ensure that the documents were in the specified order, collate and number the pages, and sew them into covers to create volumes of three to four hundred pages each. Subsequent operations on the file might lead to removing items, crossing out page numbers and renumbering.

Secret police files belong to the genre of the criminal record, but in Vatulescu's opinion, the remarkable variety of sources shows how they depart from it: officers do not simply look for evidence of a particular crime but rather examine a person's entire biography for suspect tendencies.[37] As Nicolae Steinhardt wrote, "You are not accused for what you have done, but for who you are"[38]—specifically, for being a particular kind of person: an enemy. *What kind* of enemy might vary over time: if we read a file as autobiography, it shows how the Securitate was constantly changing its view of its subjects, rewriting them repeatedly. In my case, I go from being suspected of military spying to being seen as a Hungarian in disguise, fomenting unrest among Hungarians in Cluj, to being a spy for the dissident movement—though in each of these scenarios I remain a presumed CIA agent. Because officers did not want simply to "solve" a crime but to inspect a complete life history for tell-tale patterns, no detail was insignificant: they recorded as much as possible of the person's life and activity[39]—much as an ethnographer would. (They themselves note this similarity in my file.)

Such a file is thus a product of collective authorship, engaging the efforts of many different operatives, including the archivist. As a type of writing, files have linguistic and narrative conventions peculiar to them, though like the wider corpus of Communist Party archives they are full of the characteristic "wooden language," with its ritualistic invocations (class struggle, liquidation of enemies of the people, unmasking, threat, and so on), its lack of the pronoun "I" and frequent use of passive verbs and depersonalizing constructions,[40] its military metaphors (the person under surveillance is referred to as an "obiectiv," in the sense of military objective or target), and so on. The subdivision of the file by types of action (correspondence, eavesdropping, informer reports), Vatulescu observes, produces abrupt shifts in narrative voice, juxtaposing reports by the target's close friends, for instance, with the mechanical account of her being followed. Because the narrative voice jumps around, we get a disjointed portrait of the subject.[41]

In this sense, the experience of reading one's own file is disorienting, for it lacks a single narrative thread organized as a biography (in my case, I felt compelled to rearrange the entire thing chronologically so that

55

I could find myself and my experience in it.) Better said, it *is* a biography, but not one its subject fully recognizes—and in this sense, it is a fiction. Nonetheless, Vatulescu continues, the file's heteroglossia is tamed by rigid selection patterns, as the officers' reports reduce the portrait "to a cliché from an infamous stock of characters: the spy, the saboteur, the counter-revolutionary, the terrorist, and so on"—in a word, an enemy of the state.[42] Only with changes in surveillance technology, she observes, does the cacophony of the file diminish, since the now-more-prevalent telephone wiretaps fixed a central viewpoint from a constant perspective, with other kinds of evidence arrayed around it. Although the new technology did not eliminate the need for informers, it helped to set a more impersonal tone that distinguishes files of the 1980s, say, from those of two decades earlier, while further reducing narrative coherence and progression.[43]

If a person's file has a fragmenting effect on his or her sense of identity, this is not only from the lack of a biographical narrative but from a proliferation of the file's subject, through the use of multiple code names. Each case officer assigns a code name to his target, and if a person is a target in more than one time or location, there may be code names for each. If the file is closed and later a new one is opened, it may use a new code name. Thus, I am "Folclorista"

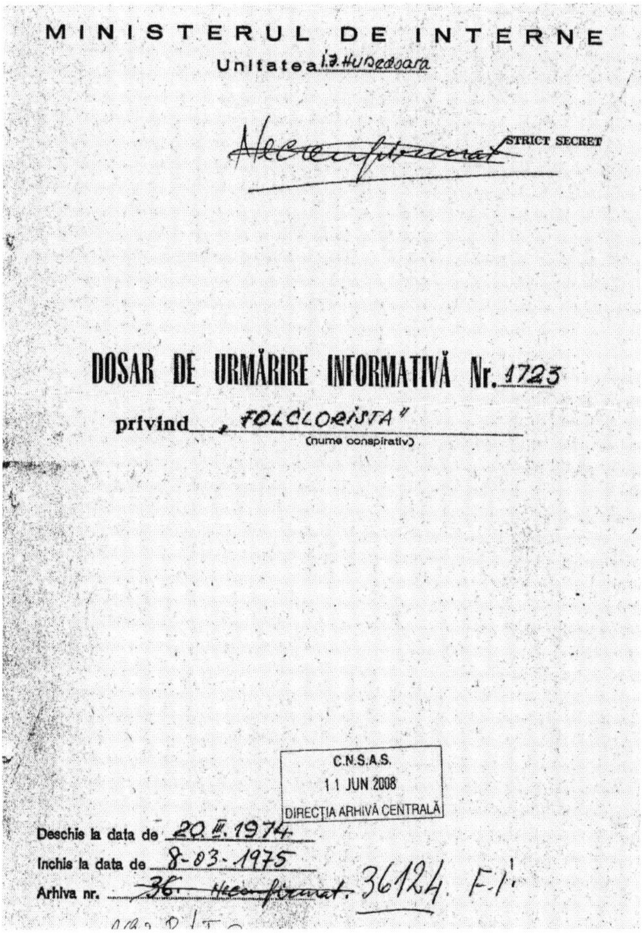

MINISTERUL DE INTERNE
Unitatea I.J. Hunedoara

~~Neconfirmat~~ STRICT SECRET

DOSAR DE URMĂRIRE INFORMATIVĂ Nr. 1723

privind „FOLCLORISTA"
(nume conspirativ)

C.N.S.A.S.
11 JUN 2008
DIRECȚIA ARHIVĂ CENTRALĂ

Deschis la data de 20.III.1974
Inchis la data de 8-03-1975
Arhiva nr. ~~36. Neconfirmat.~~ 36124. F.1.

Figure 1.5. Pseudonyms: "The FOLKLORIST," file cover page, 1974

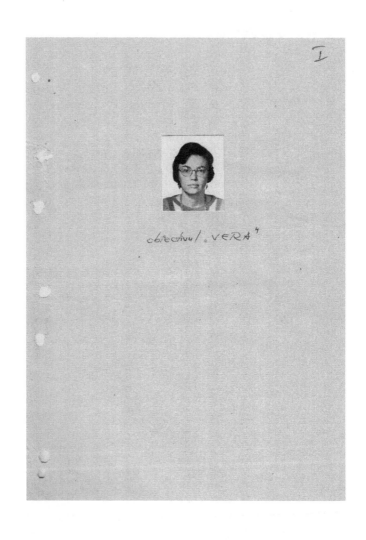

Figure 1.6. Pseudonyms: "Target VERA"

for my Hunedoara county case officers in the 1970s, "Vera" for my case officers in Cluj and Bucharest in the 1980s, "Katy" for the city of Iaşi in the late '70s and '80s, "Vanesa" for the Foreign Intelligence Service. The different services also assign code names, particularly the shadowing service: I am "Kora" for the one in Cluj, "Viky" for Timişoara, "Venera" for Hunedoara. Seven names, four of them with rich activity logs. "Disguises," indeed!

In talking of "my" file, I assume that somehow my own sense of being a constant presence across time gives unity to my piece of the archive—that is, I assume that its object unifies the file. But the object has many names and could thus be different people. Maybe I am not the same person in 1985 as in 1973; maybe the Securitate were postmodernists *avant la lettre*, recognizing that people have multiple identities. In Romanian, people refer to it as "dosarul meu," "my dossier/file," even when it contains multiple volumes from multiple years (as mine does). This takes the *ex post facto* view that a single unified human being or personality holds the whole thing together. But this is to project onto the file a unity that cannot be presumed as it is formed. When an officer is shadowing a target, he does not necessarily know "whom" he is following; likewise the person transcribing phone conversations or letters. Conspirativity—the segmentation of the Securitate labor process—thus segments the social world it appropriates.

The Files As Agents

So far I have been speaking of the Securitate and its officers as creators of the files. In this final section I will entertain the opposite question: to what extent are the files themselves social agents? Ever since the 1986 publication of Michel Callon's celebrated paper on scallop-fishing in France (which treated the scallops as actors on par with the fisherman and the conservation scientists he studied), and with the increasing popularity of actor-network theory and science studies, it has become possible to ask questions about the efficacy of objects in the world—objects such as surveillance files. What effects have these files had? I do not refer specifically to the effects of surveillance practices themselves, though they may enter into this discussion, but rather the effects of the existence of these files and the manner in which they are made, circulate, and act.

The theoretical perspective I draw upon now challenges referential theories of language. For example, Matthew Hull, who employs semiotic theory and science studies to analyze what he calls Pakistan's "government of paper," observes of the writing he finds in Pakistani government files, "graphic artifacts are not simply the instruments of already existing social organizations. Instead, their specific discourses and material forms precipitate the formation of shifting networks and groups of official and unofficial people and things."[44] I confess that this is not a way of thinking in which I am fully at home; I am still basically a referential-theory kind of person and find it difficult to hoist myself out of the assumption that when we speak, our words refer to existing things in the world. But I have decided to accept the challenge posed by Hull and others to try on something different—because the whole matter of files is itself something in which I do not feel at home. I have a file; it contains words, which ought to refer to a reality in the world. But I find the reality those words purport to represent alien, since I am their object. So to try on a *modality of analysis* in which I am uncomfortable seems just the thing. In pursuing this line of thought, I am asking questions about sources, something that historians always ask about, but I pose them in a somewhat different form.

When people from the US learn about my file, they tend to ask the same question: "did they get the truth or is it all made up, all lies?" This question points to the fact that we (or my US interlocutors, anyway) tend to take the file as an object for granted. We assume that it contains reports of various kinds, which are more or less true—that is, we posit a truth relation between the words in the file and the persons or behaviors described in them, through the agency of the officer and his paper. We posit, in other words, a referential theory of the file in relation to the reality of the person it is about, and we ask about the nature of that relation. Romanian readers of files share this assumption—as we gather, for example, from Poenaru's report of an episode witnessed one day in the CNSAS reading room. A man reading his own file "took out a pen and started to make his own annotations on the original, marking those things that were factually true and crossing out those that were false or incorrect—to the horror of the archive's guardians. This is perhaps the perfect metaphor, the extreme case, of how the files were generally read in post-communism: with an eye to their correspondence to reality."[45] He goes on to argue that this reveals two different logics to the files: the logic under which they were composed—"as 'structural biographies,' as accounts of an overall social structure comprised of many levels and interlinked plots"—and the logic of the postsocialist reading, more autobiographical and concerned with truth.[46]

Following Poenaru and Hull, it is apparent that the truth-value of what is in the file may not be the most interesting question we can entertain about it. Although we can profitably ask by what techniques and assumptions the officers produce *what they consider* its truth, as I will do in my third chapter, that is different from the more common preoccupation with whether files tell "what really happened." That preoccupation has the consequence of effacing the file itself, of reducing it to a paper form of the officer's relation to the person under surveillance. It is to avoid this that I ask about the agency of the file: what social effects does it have? What (to maintain the "fiction" of my chapter title) does it fashion? These effects include aspects of the very physicality that have been overlooked, and to which I will briefly draw attention here.

One way to begin thinking about this is through performative theories of language, which a number of scholars have found particularly persuasive for analyzing socialist societies.[47] Here is former Romanian communist and political prisoner Belu Zilber, on how he came to think about Securitate files.

The first great socialist industry was that of the production of files.... This new industry has an army of workers: the informers. It works with ultramodern electronic equipment (microphones, tape recorders, and so forth), plus an army of typists with their typewriters. Without all this, socialism could not have survived.... In the socialist bloc, people and things exist only through their files. All our existence is in the hands of him who possesses files and is constituted by him who constructs them. Real people are but the reflection of their files.... For the first time since the creation of the world demiurges have appeared on the earth. The masters of all the files are our masters, the silent fabricators of files—our creators.[48]

This puts us in mind of Ian Hacking's felicitous notion of "making up people,"[49] which, as I indicated above, was one of the Securitate's main tasks: their job was to produce the category of "enemy," including spies and various other types of enemies, and to populate it with real people. The files were a principal means of doing so, a repository containing the tracks of that process. Somehow the materiality of the file guarantees the reality/identity of the person produced through it. We can see their procedure as in part performative: by assuming that someone was an enemy or spy, they created an identity that the person was expected to perform; the officers' reports then show how they read these performances. (That they were especially likely to validate a performance as "spying" in the case of ethnographers emerges clearly from documents in the archive.[50])

Florin Poenaru offers a wonderful example of making up people in his description of how the Securitate made writer Dorin Tudoran into a dissident. Tudoran published parts of his file under the title *I, Their Son* (*Eu, fiul lor*—appropriately, for my purposes, opening it with the lines, "I didn't write this book—it wrote me"[51]). From it, Poenaru finds ample evidence for how a person who began by simply complaining about not being able to travel and not having the job he wanted is increasingly "discovered" to be a dissident: to have contacts in the West, to be writing "socio-political tracts" that are picked up by Radio Free Europe, and finally to be "at the center of a wide web of spies, French connections and illegal trade of manuscripts."[52] Finally, he is forced to emigrate (Romania's preferred way of dealing with dissidents). Poenaru concludes, "It is only by reading these files as a work of art and as detective novels that we actually reach [their] true political dimension."[53] Reinforcing this message, Tudoran's file later served as the basis for Gianina Carbunariu's theatrical production "X mm of Y km," in which the actors keep changing roles and starting over so that "ultimately, the characters, their identities and social roles are effectively suspended and what seems to matter is only the discourse, performatively creating the reality of the meeting. The content of the utterances becomes irrelevant, so does the actual identity of those doing the utterance: the text and the script prevail by virtue of their sheer repetition."[54] One is reminded, in this description, of the infamous show trials of the 1950s, which performatively turned loyal Party members into enemies of the state.

Belu Zilber's file makes him a traitor, Tudoran's makes him a dissident, mine makes me a CIA agent, and countless other people's files make them other kinds of enemy. Files can also make "informers" out of people who staunchly deny that they ever held this role. For example, the Czechoslovak StB created collaborator cards simply from making contact with someone, even if that person refused to collaborate with them. One might argue that in this kind of "making up people," the files are not fully agents but mere accomplices. Even as accomplices, however, files can act. For one thing, they can recruit people unwittingly into the service of the organization. My own file recruits me into the Securitate, making me an integral part of it even while excluding me from the file's production. So even as an American, I help to constitute the Securitate arm of the Romanian Party-state.

Let me take another approach to the agency of files by returning to the earlier discussion of conspirativity. As I indicated there, the compartmentalization of the labor process so as to maintain the secrecy of officers' identities and work practices meant that in any one location, many members of the organization were unknown to each other; this had consequences for organizational cohesion, further undermined by factionalism and backbiting that made careers unstable. A very few senior officers—each county's Securitate chief; the head of the Inspectorate for Police, Securitate, and Penal Investigations; their deputies; and the organization's top generals in Bucharest to whom they reported—were in a position to know who the operatives were and what they were doing. As Poenaru writes: "Only the top echelon of the Securitate had access to the *entire* file: the rest of the employees just contributed with only parts and pieces... . Ultimately, the file was nothing else than a huge puzzle that only a handful of people could see in its entirety."[55] Understandably, the workload of such people likely exceeded their ability to keep track of everything.

Conspirativity made the Securitate a "virtual community" ahead of its time. If the operatives involved in shadowing, censoring letters, transcribing taped conversations, and so forth were all disguised, the circulation of the material files was the principal instrument of their cohesion. Files traveled from the hands of the case officer up the hierarchy, accumulating marginal notes from various superiors on the way, and came back down with the superiors' observations and instructions, like this document with an informer's note and three levels of commentary—that of the informer's case officer, then of the officer's immediate superior, and of an even higher-level officer at the top of the page. (See Figure 1.7) Their trajectory materialized among various levels of the Securitate a conversation that would never or rarely happen in person. In this manner, Hull suggests, file circulation helps to produce collective agency and to distribute responsibility. These effects are also achieved by certain linguistic conventions that distribute authorship ambiguously (the use of passive and reflexive constructions, for example, and absence of the pronoun "I"—a common feature of ritual speech).[56] In brief, the process of their regular circulation made files complete and constituted the Securitate as an organization, a collective actor, rather than as scattered individuals writing reports. Is it going too far to say that only now, with the opening of the files, can we fully perceive that unity, as the gaze of file readers turns the Securitate and its archive into coherent, unified entities, which they were not before?

Even *without* the constraints of conspirativity one can make such an argument, as has Richard Harper in his ground-breaking study of the International Monetary Fund. Writing about staff reports, he states that their paramount function "is to act as instruments to cohere and control the organisation."[57]

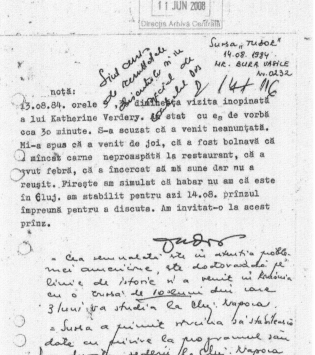

Sursa „Tudor"
14.08. 1984
MR. BURA VASILE
Nr. 0232

notă:
13.08.84. orele 9, dimineața vizita inopinată
a lui Katherine Verdery. A stat cu ea de vorbă
cca 30 minute. S-a scuzat că a venit neanunțată.
Mi-a spus că a venit de joi, că a fost bolnavă că
a mîncat carne neproaspătă la restaurant, că a
avut febră, că a încercat să mă sune dar nu a
reușit. Firește am simulat că habar nu am că este
în Cluj. am stabilit pentru azi 14.08. prînzul
împreună pentru a discuta. Am invitat-o la acest
prînz.

Figure 1.7. A document's circulation coheres its multiple readers

69

Every file has multiple authors as well as many readers; the organization tasked with setting world economic policy—or with ensuring the security of the Romanian state—uses this body of material to do so, and is itself made as a collective actor by the circulation of its files. An advantage of this line of thinking is that we do not have to accept the organization's own rationale or definition of itself in order to define it: we can look to its behavior. Such an approach helps us to *bound* the organization, by following what Harper refers to as "document careers." This is a useful reminder, given the fragmentation of the intelligence services. Where are the boundaries of the Securitate as an organization? They are indicated by the aggregate trajectories of files, which set the Securitate apart from other segments of the communist bureaucracy, into which these files rarely if ever circulated.[58]

In a fascinating discussion, Harper pushes these questions further by asking about the difference between paper and electronic files. He is not thinking only of the difference between paper that creates trajectories through its travels in the organization, on the one hand, and on the other, people who turn on a computer to access a central data bank that everyone can visit. Rather, he draws on research about differences between these two media in the kinds of embodied reading practices they entail. This work indicates that paper documents affect how readers *impute relationships* among sections of a document, allowing them "to get to grips" with it in ways that are harder with hypertext.[59] The stability of a printed text enables building a cognitive map of it more easily, and its linearity on the page facilitates building and inferring cohesion, by both author and readers. Because readers tend to make inferences based on adjacent text, hypertext can generate inferences, less likely with paper text, that the author did not intend.[60] All these considerations underscore the vital significance of the files' materiality and give special meaning to the fact that despite the Securitate's endowment with powerful computers, most of its files remained in paper rather than electronic form until the regime's end.

In case this actor-network approach to the Securitate archive seems a bit far-fetched, I will end with one final aspect of the agency of files that is incontestable: their effects in post-1989 politics. Matthew Hull quotes a Pakistani bureaucrat who told him, "Files are always ready to talk, if not now while you are in your seat then later…. Files are time bombs."[61] Almost every East European reader would surely agree with that image. These archives, unlike many government archives in the world, were never imagined to have any readers other than the security apparatus. It is one thing to ask about the archive's efficacy in the context of its own norms, including the possible effects of circulating its files. But the events of 1989 have radically recontextualized these archives, lending them effects that were never anticipated by their makers. Since 1989, files have wrecked lives, destroyed family relationships and friendships, made and broken careers in politics and other domains, sought and failed to achieve "transitional justice" and "democratization," and otherwise produced boundless mayhem as well as tremendous opportunity. They have caused profound self-doubt on the part of persons who have read their own files—leading them to ask, as I have, for instance, whether they were unwitting spies after all, and why they were so trusting of friends, spouses, or kin who informed on them.[62] The files have become sources both for generating forms of political or moral capital (as people use them to "prove" that they were not collaborators or were victimized by those who were), and for *preventing* people from acquiring it (through exposing or threatening to expose their presence in the files).[63]

Files acquire this kind of "time bomb" agency mainly if they are seen as repositories of truth. But everything we know about how the files were put together diminishes their likely truth-value. Informers reported under duress, out of malice, or inaccurately; case officers made tendentious interpretations that suited their ends; destruction of files left enormous lacunae in the corpus; agents opened files on people even when their "recruits" refused to cooperate; the demands of the planned economy set performance targets that compelled sloppy work; competition among officers and branches of the secret service aggravated that tendency; and so forth. Moreover, as Poenaru has observed, the insistence on seeing the files as matters of truth has, in a dialectical reversal, "led to the proliferation of a widespread climate of suspicion, fear and denunciation, that is, precisely of what the former Securitate was mainly blamed for and the lustration mechanisms were hoping to eliminate from the public life of post-communism. By inscribing the Securitate archive as a site of truth about the past, post-communism simply prolonged its logic into the present."[64]

* * *

The entry of the Securitate archive into contemporary postsocialist politics complicates the task of doing an ethnography of the Securitate through it, by maintaining in the present a lively sense of the harm it has wrought in Romanian society. Carlo Ginzburg, in his short piece "The Inquisitor as Anthropologist," asks why the use of Inquisition records as a source came so late. Part of his answer is that early researchers could find no religious, intellectual, or emotional identification with either the inquisitors or the defendants. In his own work with Inquisition records, he experienced growing discomfort: his emotional identification with the defendants became complicated by his growing identification with the inquisitors, whom he came to see as like ethnographers, seeking to transpose "beliefs fundamentally foreign to them into another, more unambiguous code."[65] It is more comfortable for us to assimilate the communist secret police to the inquisitor than to the ethnographer, and Ginzburg's reference to identification is wholly apt: those of us who did not participate in the communist apparatus or the police who sustained it have little or no inclination to identify with them. In part from years of oppression or Cold War propaganda, they have acquired an entirely negative image. We think of members of the Securitate, the Stasi, the ÁVH, and so forth as evil, demonic figures who broke the bones of thousands with torture and stopped the hearts of millions with fear. We are loath to see them as like anthropologists, serious practitioners of a form of inquiry.

This poses problems for doing an ethnography of the Securitate through its files. Anthropologists often seek to render the ways of "others" comprehensible by manipulating the boundaries between the strange and the familiar, comparing other people's ways with our own, as famed anthropologist Bronislaw Malinowski does in his description of the Melanesian *kula* trading ring when he compares the Trobriand Islanders' grubby shell necklaces and armbands with England's Crown Jewels.[66] To do this successfully requires developing sympathy for the ways of others so as to stand back from one's own. In this manner we defamiliarize our own cultural practices even while making strange ones more accessible, more open to identification and understanding. That technique is even more useful when one is studying one's own society, whose forms are so familiar that one cannot see them in any other light. They must somehow be "estranged," defamiliarized, so we can think about them differently.

It is difficult to adapt this procedure to work on the Securitate, however, because one resists developing sympathy for them. Anthropologist Carole McGranahan, working on an ethnography involving CIA officers, struggles to "be critical without being contemptuous" and, in her interviews with CIA agents, is uncomfortable about exposing herself to the "ethnographic seduction" that fieldwork inevitably entails.[67] Like her, I wish to understand the secret police better and will have to destabilize some of my prejudices, which I probably share with most readers from Eastern Europe, if not more widely. The technique of "estrangement" might still be useful toward this end, though,—and it has the virtue of having been developed as a literary practice by Brecht and Shklovsky in explicit relation to the practices of the secret police.[68]

In my next chapter I will try to "estrange" the Securitate by taking seriously the word "secret" in the label "secret police." I aim to sidestep some of the common-sense hatred of them in hopes of learning something that we might otherwise miss. To do so, I will present some ideas from the anthropological literature on secrecy and secret societies in places such as New Guinea and Africa, both well established in my field as rich sites for secrecy, and will follow where these ideas lead into the Securitate's secret practices.

Chapter 2

The Secrets of a Secret Police

The secret society of totalitarian regimes is the secret police.
—Hannah Arendt, *Origins.*

"Secrecy," wrote Elias Canetti, "lies at the very core of power."[1] In this he echoed Max Weber, who connected secrecy to bureaucracy: "Every bureaucracy seeks to increase the superiority of the professionally informed by keeping their knowledge and intentions secret. … Everywhere that the power interests of the domination structure toward the outside are at stake, whether it is an economic competitor of a private enterprise, or a foreign, potentially hostile polity, we find secrecy. … With the increasing bureaucratization of party organizations, this secrecy will prevail even more."[2] Anthropologist David Nugent puts the point more bluntly: "Secrecy is constitutive of social order. … Whoever succeeds in controlling secrecy has the ability to define social order."[3] It is therefore no surprise that with socialism we find what Florian Banu calls "a true cult of the secret, in which the governing had to know absolutely everything about the governed, while the latter had no right to know anything

... of the 'secrets of power.'"[4] This secrecy was most fully concentrated in the Securitate, an organization defined by what it did not share.

All modern states (and many older ones) have had their intelligence services, whose job is to purify the society in question of contaminants—to label certain behaviors or kinds of people "dangerous" and work to contain them or expel them from the polity. Since the definition of danger and its containment enjoy some similarities in practice irrespective of socio-cultural context, intelligence services have a variety of tactics in common. To call them "secret police" is something of a misnomer, though, for their existence is fully known. None of the communist organizations popularly referred to as "secret police"—East Germany's Stasi, Hungary's ÁVO/ÁVH, Romania's Securitate, Poland's UB/SB, the Soviet NKVD/KGB, and so forth—actually has the word "secret" in its title. The common thread, rather, is "security." Beginning with the Soviet *Committee for State Security* (KGB), we have Romania's *Department of State Security* (Securitate); Hungary's *State Protection Authority* (ÁVH/ÁVO, later III/III), East Germany's *Ministry for State Security* (Stasi), Poland's *Security Department* (UB) or *Security Service* (SB), and so forth.[5] Security is not necessarily based on the kind of repression assumed by the secret; it is thought of as a positive outcome, a creation or furthering of order. But clearly the kind of security the secret police of socialism were after made multiple uses of secrets, hence their popular name.

To think about secrecy is a conceptual challenge, rather like trying to theorize silence: how can we think about an absence? Silence can reflect many things: a willful suppression, or a simple lack of anything to say, or a lack of conviction that one is *entitled* to have something to say,[6] or the presence of a doxa or hegemonic ideology that makes some things unthinkable/unsayable. The silence itself does not tell us which of these options to explore. Secrecy—with silence as its instrument—is similar. Karma Lochrie likens secrecy to dark matter in physics, which "occupies the invisible realm of physical properties, like the spaces between stars. To try to talk about secrets is something like trying to describe [those] spaces."[7] Sissela Bok, in her widely cited work *Secrets*, finds it impossible to offer a single definition of them. She sees the secret's defining trait as hiding or concealment, keeping something intentionally hidden, and she includes both the thing hidden (usually information) and the methods used to conceal it.[8] For many, she notes, secrecy has negative associations, such as for former US President Woodrow Wilson, who once said, "Secrecy means impropriety."[9] The fundamental assumption of western democracies that government should be transparent complicates any attempt to write about secret police in a neutral manner. At the same time, however, the norm of transparency produces a *frisson* at its transgression, giving us pleasure in the secret.

In this chapter I will explore the Securitate and its secrets, approaching it from several different angles loosely centering on a basic conundrum that emerges from my research so far.[10] On the one hand, the Securitate effectively kept its secrets from the public and maintained a climate of fear and anxiety among them. On the other, as I indicated in the previous chapter and will further show here, what we can glimpse of its inner workings—or can speculate about them by analogy with other kinds of cases—suggests some major inefficiencies that must surely have compromised the organization's effectiveness. How are we to put these two things together: the sometimes-chaotic view from inside the organization and the fearful view from the populace? Secrecy was the membrane separating them. East Europeans certainly took their secret police seriously, many with good reason, and evidence abounds of the fear the secret police aroused in them. But émigré writer Nicolae Corbeanu writes of his four years as an informer, which ended when a colleague offered him the following advice: "Don't give them any more notes, not even token ones. Don't meet with them any more. Interrupt all contact….

Nothing will happen to you, I guarantee it.... If you knew what miserable shitheads they are in fact, you wouldn't be so afraid of them."[11] Corbeanu followed the advice, and in a couple of months the officer stopped calling him; he suffered no repercussions. After he left Romania for Germany in 1973, he repeatedly asked himself why he had agreed to become an informer. His answer: the terror the Securitate inspired in people, with its sinister and terrifying reputation for pure arbitrariness.[12]

Although I do not have space here to augment my ethnography of the Securitate with the popular reactions to it, Corbeanu's experience helps to set my agenda for this chapter. How can we get behind the Securitate's fearsome image, and what happens if we do? Does discovering the organization's inner workings and its inefficiencies negate the mystique of secrecy on which it feeds—rather like Dorothy's encounter with the Wizard of Oz? I cannot fully answer these questions but will run several sorties into them, hoping to illuminate further the workings of the organization and the place of secrecy in it. First, I consider secrecy as a matter of its *content*, the information or other thing that is hidden, and then in terms of its *social-structural and cultural relations* of exclusion and inclusion. Here I include some evidence concerning the lives of secret police agents. Secrecy is also a matter of *practices and technologies*: *how* the thing is hidden or the flow of information controlled—or (avoiding the language of content) what codes it employs to exclude and to limit access. Finally, I discuss some of secrecy's *effects,* which bring me back to the Securitate's fearsomeness. These various approaches are useful precisely because of the conceptual challenge of dealing with an absence: we have to try numerous angles in order to discern what is there.[13] Because these four aspects vary according to the kind of society in which secrecy is being practiced, I will try to specify what is peculiar to socialism about the forms we find.

Following a brief discussion of the content of the Securitate's secrets, I embark on a somewhat unorthodox comparison of some social-structural aspects using anthropological literature on secrecy and secret societies.[14] My hope is to learn something new about the secret police but also to disrupt our accustomed way of thinking about it. How does the anthropology of secrecy enable us to move inside the Securitate ethnographically and away from its frightening reputation? Perhaps the secret societies of New Guinea and Africa will put things in a fresh light. I recognize that my procedure has a number of drawbacks, not least of them being the huge gap in the nature and social complexity of the cases I am comparing. Although some might argue that comparisons with early modern religious and secular brotherhoods, professional guilds, or military organizations might be more relevant,[15] I believe that going farther afield gives me more insight into the social structure (as opposed to the origins) of Securitate secrecy and helps me avoid becoming mired in questions about the "truth" of the files.[16]

The Content of Secrets

Let me begin with a question about content: What *were* the secrets of the Securitate? Despite a public imaginary convinced that the archives contain a wealth of secrets, scholars of these organizations like to say, "The secret is that there was no secret." In fact, however, there were many. There were the secrets of the organization's own work practices: the true identities of targets, officers, and informers, the fact that certain people were under surveillance, the passwords used to make contact, the targets and informers a given officer was working with and the kind of work he[17] was doing with them, the very fact that a person worked for the Securitate, the contents of informers' reports, and so forth. That there were hidden microphones overhearing one's conversations, that mail was censored for the general populace, that people were shadowed—these facts were supposed to be secret, though everyone knew them. Also secret was the ongoing verification of not only targets but informers as well, by eavesdropping, shadowing, censorship of their mail, and so on. These and many other secrets of the Securitate's labor process center on the demands of conspirativity—the compartmentalization of work that I mentioned in chapter 1—which made secrets of relations with other officers, with informers, and with family and friends.

There were also military secrets and, as my own file reveals, secrets concerning the workings of socialism that the apparatus feared outsiders like me might uncover and publicize—such as the existence of an informal economy, or popular dissatisfaction, or bad relations among national groups, and so forth. Certain things in one's workplace might be designated state secrets, though it seems that Romanians were to divine on their own what was secret and protect it. (For example, although I did not understand it at the time, I recall the consternation that greeted my request in 1973 for a map of the county I was to work in: might it be a state secret, my grant officer wondered?) Overlapping with these were secrets contained in official documents: all those items marked "top secret" in the archives of both the Party bureaucracy and the Securitate itself. There were three levels of secrecy for these: "top secret of exceptional importance," "top secret," and "secret." Issues of the magazine *Securitatea*, launched in 1968 as an internal bulletin to help the apparatus of state security improve their work methods and educational level, contained a note specifying that the magazine must be used according to the rules of top secret documents: it must not be taken out of Securitate offices, and copying its contents was strictly forbidden. Instructions from higher to lower levels in the apparatus were secret, as were training manuals. At the Securitate school, former officer Victor Mitran reports, students acquiring different skills (counterespionage, shadowing, and so on) were not allowed to talk with one another about what they were learning.[18] Florian Banu writes of the proliferating "secret" designations for documents not just in the Securitate but in the Party bureaucracy as a whole, a habit one government minister attributed to a desire to avoid responsibility.[19] Ann Stoler has observed, "State sovereignty resides in the power to designate arbitrary social facts of the world as matters of security."[20] Romania's Party-state made liberal use of this form of sovereignty.

Among the biggest secrets was the secret whose existence the Securitate's work assumed: they were not the secret POLICE but the SECRET police, hunting down secrets. They were convinced that secrets existed among the citizenry, secrets that would unmask a hidden enemy, a saboteur, a spy, a counterrevolutionary, a danger to the state or Party. Such secrets were potentially everywhere, both "out there" in the world and "in here" in the Party apparatus. Uncovering them was the Securitate's raison d'être, toward maintaining social order. Sometimes the secrets were of modest import, gathered instrumentally to use in recruiting people as informers—the secret of an illicit affair, an illegally terminated pregnancy, an attempted bribe, or something stolen from one's workplace. Collecting these secrets enabled the recruiters to throw potential informers off balance, proving to them that "we know everything." Officers would propose to *keep* these things secret in exchange for the person's gathering information.

Related to and underlying all these secrets was the "state secret"—its substance a virtual secret, since Romania's 1971 law on it gave almost no information on what it meant.[21] The only hint was wording in article 5, which referred to data concerning the production plan, investments, labor force, and means of production, as well as those referring to actual or prospective production capacity (all of which were usually presented in percentages rather than raw numbers). As Hungarian-Romanian philosopher István Király states, in his meditation on the secret, Romania's laws concerning the state secret did not regulate secrets "according to their contents, but only toward ensuring their defense through procedures, interdictions, and sanctions…. Therefore, [the legislation] stands out above all for its lack of content, which confers upon it a generality and an abstraction peculiar to it."[22] By not specifying secret contents, Király argues, "Romanian communist legislation opened the way for a proliferation of the category of the secret unimaginable in other conditions."[23] Inspecting this legislation over time, he discerns a systemic tendency in socialism for the "state secret" to become secrecy's dominant form. Its endless proliferation resulted not simply from central dictates but from empowering *all* socialist state and community organizations to designate things as secret, thereby offering them the key to dealing with constant pressure from production plans: they could make secret the figures they reported. Thus, the fundamental secret became the fact that the figures were false.[24]

The hunt for secrets could go to absurd lengths. Former Securitate penal interrogator Gheorghe Coțoman writes, for example, on the scandal surrounding Transcendental Meditation (TM) in the 1980s, which resulted in the arrests of numerous people including top intellectuals who had participated in some introductory TM workshops. According to Coțoman, the Securitate grew suspicious because participants would not reveal their *mantra*, having been instructed that it would lose its efficacy if they did. "Did it represent, in fact, a password with which those who received it could be contacted any time and by anyone, thereafter unhesitatingly executing the orders they received? Was there a common mantra for each socio-professional category, which would then act together in a certain direction demanded 'from above'?" Finally an officer succeeded in getting someone to give him a mantra, but he never believed that it was the real one.[25] Knowing that there really was a secret, the Securitate went berserk, wildly overreacting—at great cost to the people caught up in the scandal. This was just one of thousands and thousands of "secrets" the Securitate pursued in its job as the SECRET police.

From the literature on secrecy in such places as Africa and New Guinea, we know that underlying their secret societies is a kind of "Ur-secret" representing what the community most fears, often in the form of a monstrous and terrifying creature they must appease with rituals (the *Marsalai* or *Nggwal* of New Guinea Tambaran cults, for instance). Although some scholars have dismissed this Ur-secret as a fabrication, that criticism is unacceptable: *all* our life as human beings in society rests on fabrications, starting, some would say, with the idea of God. Our job as social analysts is to understand the fabrications, and to ask how they spread within a community and with what consequences. Anikó Szűcs suggests that just as in African and New Guinea secret societies, the Party leaders and secret police of Soviet communism fabricated an "Ur-secret," the root of all fears: namely, the "enemy within," from which the country could purify itself only through secret ritual operations.[26] Sometimes, of course, that enemy was "real": actual human beings attempting to sabotage the revolution. Even if all known enemies could be exterminated, however, the enemy as *potential* would still exist. For the Securitate, uncovering that secret potential and extirpating it went hand in hand with its fabrication.

They organized themselves around that secret through secret societies. I am hardly the first person to have this thought. Hannah Arendt, citing Alexandre Koyré,[27] wrote in *The Origins of Totalitarianism*, "The secret society of totalitarian regimes is the secret police." She notes that both Hitler and Stalin had been members of secret societies before they became totalitarian leaders, and that Hitler had written extensively on the pros and cons of secret societies as models for the Nazi movements.[28] Closer to my own field is Armenian anthropologist Levon Abrahamian's paper entitled "The Secret Police as a Secret Society."[29] I accept the challenge of this parallel and will seek to fill out an understanding of it, toward offering an ethnography of Securitate secrecy.

89

Secrecy as a Social-Structural and Cultural System

Anthropologists have been thinking about secrecy and secret societies from the outset, beginning with research on Iroquois Indians by the "founder" of US anthropology, Lewis Henry Morgan, and proceeding with work on secret societies around the world.[30] Characteristic of this literature is that unlike much of the writing in sociology or political science, it does not presume the individual as the bearer of secrets, privilege the realm of the "private" as a space of secrecy, or assume transparency as the norm. The most extensive elaboration of these ideas comes from New Guinea specialist and secrecy theorist Gilbert Herdt, who finds in New Guinea men's secret cults positive sources of meaning and identity (rather than the instruments of female oppression and peculiarly transgressive sexuality more often described for them).[31]

This rich and varied literature has a number of themes, largely concerning the social and cultural relations of secrecy. They include the connection of secrecy to power structures and politics; its role in initiation (with implications for meaning, identity, and solidarity among the initiates); its creation of an alternative reality; and its relationship to social change. I begin with secrecy and power politics. Like numerous modern forms such as nationalism and citizenship,

90

secrecy as a cultural form implies insiders and outsiders: those who profess to know, and those who do
not. Herdt writes, "Secrecy is an intentional process
of differentiating included persons and entities from
those excluded, while simultaneously building solidarity among secret-sharers.... Secret collectives as-
semble hierarchies, between outsiders and insiders."[32]
Like members of other secret societies, *Securiști* were
graded according to the degree of secret knowledge
to which they had access—a function of the principle of conspirativity. Everyone was to know only as
much as was absolutely necessary to doing his job.
The lowly informer knew nothing beyond the information he gathered; he did not even know who else
was informing. The operatives engaged in following,
eavesdropping, opening correspondence, and so forth
did not know what other information was being collected, and they might not even know the identity
of the person they were following; only the case officer knew that—and they might not know his identity, either. Senior officers further up the hierarchy
saw everything: the reports of the case officers, including at least some of the evidence supporting their
conclusions, as well as the opinions of intermediate
and superior officers concerning the case. The top officers also knew the full contours of the surveillance
effort, who was doing what; officers lower down did

not know this, as I indicated in my example (chapter 1) of a Securitate officer's photograph in my surveillance file.

In the ethnographic literature, secrecy is always coupled with hierarchy. According to William Murphy, an eminent scholar of the Kpelle of Liberia famed for their secret societies, "The secret is essentially a boundary mechanism separating members of different social categories or groups…. In Kpelle society secrecy separates elders from youth."[33] Elsewhere he writes, "Leaders of the secret societies claim to have esoteric knowledge of medicines, history, and various other specialties important to Kpelle life. Through these claims, secret societies enable powerful community elders to control the labor and services of youthful clients, who are taught to be dependent on the esoteric knowledge of their elders. The politics of creating dependent clients through secret societies is a feature of a more general process in which power, authority, and wealth derive largely from controlling dependent wives, children, relatives, clients, and other followers."[34] In other words, the Kpelle were a "patronage" society based, like socialist societies, on accumulating not *wealth in things* but *wealth in people*.[35]

Murphy's analysis raises for us the question, Were secrecy rules of the Securitate a means by which senior officers collected clients—perhaps insulating them from the competitive patronage of other Party leaders *outside* the Securitate organization? And were the rules of conspirativity within the Securitate partly aimed at maintaining hierarchy, as the ethnographic literature might suggest? Hazelrigg observes, "The more extensive the secrecy of the secret society, the greater the tendency toward centralization of authority,"[36] and Gusterson summarizes a larger literature showing that in organizations practicing secrecy, "compartmentalization of knowledge consolidates the power of senior members over their subordinates, who are less well informed."[37] Although the reason given for conspirativity rules was to preserve the cover of officers and informers, they also had the effect of reinforcing inequality within the organization.

As Murphy indicates, the most common means for creating boundaries between those with and without secret knowledge is through communicating it selectively. Among people like the Kpelle, those having knowledge (elders) gave it out gradually to juniors, most often as part of complex and often lengthy processes of initiation, capped by secrecy oaths never to reveal the knowledge to outsiders or other noninitiates (normally, in these instances, women). The process can be laden with political strategy: we see this for example in Richard Price's book *First-Time*, which offers an unusually detailed picture of it for the Saramaka maroons of the Suriname rain forest, and in Beryl Bellman's *The Language of Secrecy*, about the metaphors, symbols, and procedures through which secret knowledge is communicated in the Poro secret society in Liberia.[38] As Urban puts it, the procedures and tactics "by which social agents conceal or reveal, hoard or exchange, certain valued information [make secrecy] a discursive strategy that transforms a given piece of knowledge into a scarce and precious resource, a valuable commodity, the possession of which in turn bestows status, prestige, or symbolic capital on its owner."[39]

Initiation into the Securitate occurred at two levels, at least: one for new officers, and one for informers. After 1960, most new officers were initiated through training courses at the Securitate school in Bucharest. There, according to the memoir of former officer Victor Mitran, they underwent rigors like that of army "boot camp" to teach them to endure the most terrible frustrations, reinforced by long hours of political education that formed a specific world view, structured around the mortal danger Romania faced from its omnipresent enemies.[40] Training a field operative involved gradually communicating to him the secrets of surveillance work. At his induction, he signed a loyalty oath not to reveal them, which might read something like this, sworn by one of my own case officers

at his induction: "I swear strictly to preserve state secrets and under no circumstances to divulge the actions of the State Security organs. I will fight for the
destruction of all spies, saboteurs, diversionists, and
all those others who make an attempt on state security or rise up against the construction of socialism in
the Romanian Socialist Republic."[41]

To think of these training procedures as aspects
of initiation into a secret society places them in an
unusual light, emphasizing the hierarchical transmission of secret knowledge and of patterns of sociality,
common to secret societies elsewhere.[42] Although one
might object that in most secret societies this knowledge is esoteric whereas here it is not, I would disagree: many of the things an officer-in-training had
to learn for his work indeed had an esoteric quality.[43] Securitate initiation also involved the transmission of relational patterns and socialities, inculcating
a reflexive respect for hierarchy as well as solidarity
among the initiates. We know little about the consequences of initiation for identities, aside from General Neagu Cosma's observations about the effects of
their training on the recruits' world view, "detach-
ing us from our way of thinking and understanding life up to then and introducing us to a world of
the fantastic."[44] Unlike initiation rituals in places like
New Guinea, which had the creation of masculini-

ty as their central aim, masculine identity in Securitate initiation was probably just a result of predominantly male socialization. But it is possible, as Julie Fedor reports for the Cheka and its successors in the Soviet Union, that this socialization served to consolidate patriotic identities around the figure of the "enemy" and the need to purify the nation of contaminants.[45] Former officer Constantin Bucur describes, for instance, the tremendous energy his superiors put into whipping up hatred among his officer training cohort toward the anticommunist partisans fighting in the mountains—years after the last partisan had been eliminated.[46] The special formation of Securitate officers is brought into relief by the comment of someone who completed a regular university degree before he was hired to teach new recruits, and who reported to me that in his unit, the word was, "Be careful of him, he wasn't formed by us, so he's not trustworthy."

The memoirs of retired Securitate generals Neagu Cosma and Tănase Evghenie describe another feature of a *Securist*'s life that was like an ongoing initiation ordeal: the permanent verification (that is, surveillance) to which such officers were subjected throughout their careers.[47] Cosma's cohort of new recruits found themselves increasingly aware of being verified, and when he complained to the teacher/leader of the training course, "He confirmed to me that we are under special attention but it would be good to get used to it, since this is part of our new profession—for our whole lives we will be under surveillance by both our own side and that of the enemy we will confront."[48] Cosma gives the rule of silence imparted by their superiors to all recruits: "All the secrets gathered between these walls are to remain here. Nothing is more grave in our work than to let secrets fly at will. We must be vigilant! And vigilance means not to tell someone else what you *think* can be said, only what *must* be said."[49]

The initiation of informers and other collaborators was rather different.[50] An officer recruited an informer after long preparation, during which he would learn as much as possible about the candidate and determine the strategy most likely to succeed: appeals to patriotism, material incentives, blackmail on the basis of illegal or compromising behavior, and so on. One or two officers would make the approach. The initial recruitment could last for hours, days, or weeks, even longer—one informer reported in a CNSAS interview that her recruitment had lasted nine months: a true initiation ordeal for the candidate.[51] Following it the case officer was to keep a very close eye on the recruit's behavior and actions, for (according to the directives officers received) informers usually go through a psychic crisis following their recruitment and have to be brought back down to their normal state, so the officer should meet with them every two to four days for a while.[52] The two informers with whom I have discussed their recruitment reported that they did indeed undergo a terrible crisis, based in their direct encounter with the frightening power of the Party-state.

If the candidate agreed to become an informer, he would spend several months in a "novice" status, during which he was trained in tactics, the kinds of observation and analysis his officer required, how to write reports, and so forth. He would then be invited to full informer status—an occasion that might be marked, officer Victor Mitran writes, by a festive air, the officer and his superior wearing suits and ties, and serving coffee, food, and cognac. The candidate would write out his pledge to serve the organization in secret; "then followed the baptism," in which—very much as in secret societies the world over—the initiate would either choose or be given a new name.[53] In addition, he would sign a loyalty oath that read something like this: "I pledge not to divulge anything in connection with the activity of this secret collaboration, regardless of the person, function, or grade of kinship."[54] With this he separated himself from other claims on his loyalty, as initiation rituals often do.

The system of initiation into the Securitate, then, involved a two-step graded process, one for turning ordinary citizens into officers and another for turning citizens into willing or unwilling informers, the lowest rung in the hierarchy of this secret society. In both, the recruit was initiated into the mysteries of the organization by a more experienced member, whether through a training course that might involve several other officer-recruits or through the one-on-one relation of officer to informer. Both were marked by the signature acts of secret societies: a loyalty oath and one or more new names. The two recruitments were interlinked, for an informer's recruitment launched him on a long-term pedagogical relation with the officer, rather like the long apprenticeships in some secret societies. And like initiation for officers, that for informers involved constant surveillance to verify that they were not divulging secrets and were "sincere" in their work, a constant concern.

The new names were part of another feature common to secret societies worldwide: the fabrication of an alternative reality. Arendt captured this habit of fabrication when she remarked sardonically, "Totalitarianism in power ... establishes the secret police as the executors and guardians of its domestic experiment in constantly transforming reality into fiction."[55] In his celebrated paper on secrecy, Georg Simmel wrote: "The secret offers the possibility ... of a second world alongside the manifest world."[56] This second world is an essential feature of the Securitate's regime of secrecy—as anyone who has examined a surveillance file can attest, especially if the file is one's own. Secrecy guards the portal of this parallel world, allowing easier movement across it and enabling officers to "acquire identities far more dramatic than those of their daily lives, identities in which they have great power and influence."[57] The fabrication begins with the pseudonyms that conspirativity requires for informers and targets, as well as for the secret places in which officers meet their informers.[58] Additional pseudonyms for the target come from various operatives engaged in one or another part of the surveillance project, as I indicated in the previous chapter. Only the case officers know whom all these names refer to. Thus, people entering the world of a surveillance file are rebaptized, often several times over, and become unrecognizable to anyone else. Moreover, conspirativity also requires of both officers and informers the constant invention of fictions—about who they are, what they are doing, where they are going, their occupations, why they are talking together in a particular place, and so on. In Romania, these justifications are aptly known as "legends" (*legende*).

An additional trait of this fictional universe was the interpretive grid applied to the information gathered, which utilized set narrative possibilities and characters: spies, enemies of the Party, saboteurs, and so on. These figures were imagined rather like the evil spirits of New Guinea or African secret cults; the job of Securitate priest/officers was, as Levon Abrahamian puts it for the Armenian secret police, "hunting down, unmasking, and executing secret wizards (saboteurs) and enemies."[59] Whether those evil spirits really *were* dangerous was less important than that they be tracked, managed, brought under control. Because Securitate officers had to assume the targeted "enemy" was guilty, all action taken against him or her was by definition heroic. Retired General Tănase Evghenic's memoir cites the leaders' dictum, "The State Security constitutes the sharpened sword of the proletarian dictatorship," which gave officers a powerful sense of engaging in an extraordinary activity.[60]

In his work on secret societies in New Guinea, Gilbert Herdt sees their fabrication of alternative worlds as fundamental to the creation of meaning for New Guinea men, with secrecy as a powerful means of making and breaking bonds. Moreover, he argues, secrecy is vital in their affective life: it elicits excitement, shame, awe, and passion, arousing fantasy and the pleasure that accompanies it. Luhrmann, writing about secret societies of magicians in England, agrees: "Secrecy is exciting. Magicians revel in their activities, of which few outsiders know. The excitement seems a central feature of secrecy."[61] Any reader of spy novels knows that an agent's life is very exciting, but I am also thinking at a less elevated level, where the meaningfulness of one's work and activities resides.

As I know from my own file, speculations concerning the target's behavior could involve considerable flights of imagination as well as plenty of excitement. Even the smallest datum could be given unexpected significance (such as when an officer writes that they have found in my room a conference paper I gave that is—contrary to their expectations—"favorable to Romania," and his superior officer adds the marginal note, "Have you considered that she left it there for us *on purpose?*").[62] That is, they integrate themselves into my intentionality in exciting ways, regardless of my actual intentions. Of particular interest is anything having to do with the target's sexuality: who the target is sleeping with, what perverse inclinations she might have, and so on. The logic behind this interest, which drives so many spy films, was that the deepest secrets were most likely to be found in the target's most private behavior, so if the police could seduce the target or find a person intimately involved with him or her, that person was likely to learn what the target was "really" doing—learn her secret. But surveillance reports often luxuriated in such tidbits of information well beyond this logic, passing them up the hierarchy—such as with one unfortunate journal entry of mine about a night of love, which ended up on the desk of the deputy head of counterespionage in Bucharest. Tabajdi and Ungváry likewise, reporting on surveillance of a far left group in Hungary, noted that officers also used the information they collected to satisfy their thirst for gossip.[63]

Then there is the special cachet of being empowered to produce documents with those exciting words, "SECRET" and "TOP SECRET." To titillation of this kind we can add the intrigue of putting on disguises, hiding officers' identities from those around them via forms of masking, which is very common with secret societies in other contexts. The disguises included simple "masking" by anonymity (possible only in large-scale systems where impersonal interactions are the rule) and taking off one's Securitate uniform so as to pass unnoticed.[64] Most of these forms of adventure were restricted to officers, however, and denied to lowly informers. Masks and disguises took on special significance in the context of a conspiratorial ideation that saw enemies in disguise everywhere and sought to "unmask" them.

From these and other stimulating activities, the Securitate's parallel world was filled with many sources of excitement, pleasure, and confident self-realization. The memoir of officer Mitran shows a young man from a modest family who had a taste for adventure and liked to read detective novels, fascinated by the world they opened to him. When he was called into his high-school director's office one day for recruitment to become a Securitate officer, he felt "paralyzed—out of pleasure. Electrified." The recruiter put a pistol on the table and said, "'Like it? You too can have one. It's an extraordinary job, you can be an agent, a spy, you can annihilate Romania's enemies...'"[65] Behind this thrilling prospect lay secrecy. Given that many operatives (especially in the early decades) had come from humble circumstances or grinding poverty and often lacked one or both parents, this feature of their work life may have been especially meaningful to them. Secrecy supported the officers' sense of having a special mission: the defense of the Romanian nation, whose purity they would protect by finding and expelling hidden enemies, pollutants, sources of contamination. This imagery, found in secret police fiction by Romanian authors such as Pavel Coruţ,[66] joins the Securitate to the long "chekist" tradition described by Julie Fedor.[67] It would appear from articles in the publication *Vitralii—Lumini şi Umbre* (Stained-glass windows—Light and shadow), put out post-1989 by veterans of the intelligence services, that this sense of excitement and adventure marks officers' retrospective sense of their life in the Securitate.

The Ecology of Secret Societies

What brings secret societies into existence, and what makes people join them? Although an easy answer to this for the Securitate would be, "the Red Army," I will explore additional possibilities concerning secrecy in relation to social change. I am less interested in what happens to secret cults like those in New Guinea under the press of westernization[68] than in the conditions that make them adaptive in the first place. For this purpose I single out Gilbert Herdt's ideas, which I find interestingly if improbably relevant to my subject. Attempting a theory of secret societies and the conditions that produce them, Herdt points to the circumstances in which they likely appeared in New Guinea: endemic instability and male warfare, in which alliances among men were crucial but the trust essential to consolidating them was difficult to achieve. He argues: "in certain times and places, … the unstable character of social relations creates such anxiety and mistrust that it is impossible to make mutual plans and goals for social adaptation between male compatriots. Profound disruptions across generations of males made social relations conditional. In times of war and violence, the inability to predict allies or to trust colleagues led to great misfortunes and social disasters…. This social chaos and human calamity led to the use of secret ritu-

105

al initiation practices."[69] Justifying secrecy as necessary to prevailing in war, therefore, New Guinea men elaborated complex secret cults, which then spread widely across the island.

Herdt does not rest with New Guinea, however, but extends his argument to nineteenth-century upstate New York, where a young Lewis Henry Morgan was deeply involved with secret societies—both those of the Iroquois Indians he studied and those of his white compatriots (including some he founded himself).[70] It was a time when many new secret societies were forming, especially for upwardly mobile middle-class men who rejected older orders such as Freemasonry: by 1896, 5.5 million of 19 million American males, or almost 30 percent, belonged to secret societies, and some estimates place the number at closer to 40 percent.[71] Often adopting a kinship idiom, their members had to pledge loyalty through "adoption degrees" to fictive brothers and fathers, creating male camaraderie by hiding their rituals of solidarity from women. In Herdt's view, these secret societies offered a solution to problems of a specific moment in class and gender transformation in the U.S., which produced a crisis of masculinity. The rising position of women in the middle class, the suffragist movement, new ideas of an autonomous social self and individuality—all constituted challenges to men's lives and led to a perception of declining male authority. Moreover, increasing competition in the marketplace frayed existing forms of solidarity and intimacy among men. As a result, they developed new forms of collective male secrecy, which reorganized men's relations of trust and hierarchy in those uncertain times.

In brief, then, Herdt's theory of secrecy understands male secret societies as a response to major social transformations in gender and class relations, which will have different configurations in different places but concern the same basic problem, for which secrecy is a major solution: how to build trust among men in unstable circumstances. His ideas illuminate certain features of Securitate history and raise fascinating possibilities for further thought. Consider the following points about historical context, building upon the history and interorganizational environment of the Securitate from my Introduction.

1. The Soviet NKVD/KGB had set up Romania's intelligence apparatus, and for the next several decades General Secretaries Gheorghiu-Dej and Ceaușescu struggled for greater independence on three fronts: independence of Romania from the Soviets, of the Securitate from the KGB, and of the Romanian Party from the Securitate. Beginning with Ceaușescu in 1965, the organization's higher echelons were

more fully Romanianized (having been heavily Jewish and Hungarian at the beginning, with undercover NKVD/KGB officers as well).

2. Romania had had a well organized fascist movement during the 1930s. Because of the Communist Party's initially small size, its leaders had invited members of the fascist movement to join it; for the same reason, they had retained many people from the previous administration in the new state bureaucracy. Even before it began the persecution of "kulaks," the bourgeoisie, and other enemies of the people, then, the Party's own actions had surrounded it with "enemies" to be purged, giving the Securitate plenty of work to do. Surveillance was generalized, involving not just the Securitate over the population but the Securitate over its own members and over the Party, Party cadres over each other, citizens over other citizens and over cadres.[72]

3. During the 1940s and early '50s, the landscape of Eastern Europe was fairly bubbling with agents from various intelligence services. Alongside Soviet and German agents were others from the US, Britain, and France—which, even though allied with the Soviets in the war, were constantly preoccupied with getting better information. Romania was a central location for it and Romanian intelligence agents a prime target for attempted recruitment.[73]

4. Throughout Romanian society there was tremendous opposition to the communist takeover. Not only the fascists but people all over the country dragged their feet on communist initiatives, "waiting for the Americans."[74] Well into the 1950s, partisan groups maintained armed opposition in the mountains, and peasants fiercely resisted the collectivization of agriculture right up to its completion in 1962.[75] Crucially, many of these groups were organized rather like secret societies, making competing claims on people through loyalty oaths. Anticommunist partisan groups such as *Cruce și Spadă* (Cross and sword) required members to swear an oath on the Bible that they would have a soldier's devotion to the cause and never divulge the secret of the organization's existence. The fascists had used similar oaths, and some peasant traditions required them too.[76]

5. In this environment, the communists and their police turned readily to forming secret organizations, from the Party's years as an illegal movement based in secrecy. Király argues that even after the movement became legal, it retained the traces of its former self, always anxious about being destroyed if it failed to preserve the secret of its existence. In communist cosmology, then, the secret retained a privileged place, having a special attraction.[77]

109

Without doubt, trust and loyalty among men were constant problems. In such a context I find it very plausible to consider the Securitate as a secret society oriented to a landscape pulsating with rival organizations of similar type. To indicate that this is not a wholly crazy idea: before the 1989 revolution, Securitate officer Virgil Măgureanu, who later became head of Romania's post-1989 intelligence services (SRI), published some work on the Vrancea communal-property secret societies—a topic that had fascinated the Securitate from the 1950s, when those societies had supported the largest peasant uprising against collectivization.[78] Let me explore the parallels further, considering the Securitate as a secret society that operated in a field of competing organizations, many of them secret, and at the same time not completely trusting any of them—not even the apparatus of the Romanian Communist Party. My argument concerns primarily the incentives for men, not women, to participate in this overwhelmingly male organization.

Herdt's description of the conditions for secret societies in nineteenth-century New York strikes me as relevant to those in which many of Romania's men found themselves in the late 1940s and early '50s. Like men in New Guinea, they were emerging from a period of endemic warfare into one of profound so-

110

cial change. From that circumstance as well as from their Soviet counselors, they carried deep distrust of all around them, including their own Party leaders. Romania's communist "revolution" had many enemies, just like the Bolsheviks, about whom Getty and Nauman remind us, "This was a political system in which even Politburo members carried revolvers.... the Stalinists always believed themselves figuratively surrounded, constantly at war with powerful and conniving opponents."[79] The communists' goals made it clear that some form of warfare would continue for some time to come—against the kulaks, the peasants, the bourgeoisie—yet pervasive factionalism and uncertainty made it impossible to know who one's allies were. Indeed, the aftermath of World War II offered fertile ground for generating the "Ur-secret" of the feared and unknown enemies arrayed against Romania.

In a landscape full of groups opposing the new Party leadership, many of them organized in something like secret societies and seeking to bind their members through loyalty oaths, competition for members must have been great, especially given all the wartime deaths. Moreover, as in nineteenth-century New York, socialism was introducing greater equality into class and gender relations, increasing the position of women at the expense of the authority of men; extensive social mobility disrupted established forms of male solidarity. All of this would have provoked crises of masculinity or self-concept for many men.[80] In that context, Gilbert Herdt's question—How do men build trust among themselves when the conditions are wholly opposed to it?—seems very apt. Communist opposition to Freemasonry precluded that option but other kinds of secret societies offered a possible solution, whether the Communist Party, partisan groups, the fascists, or village groups that also required male solidarity, loyalty oaths, and so on. The "secret society" being set up by the NKVD/KGB offered yet another option.

From the anthropology of secrecy we learn that what counts is not the content of a secret but the structure it is embedded in. Although we're used to thinking of the basic structural opposition in socialism as that separating the Party from the rest of society, "Us" from "Them," this imagery of multiple secret organizations in competitive interaction invites us to consider other important oppositions, such as the KGB-controlled Securitate versus the increasingly nationalistic Romanian Communist Party. The Party apparatus, too, made liberal use of secrecy, closing its meetings to non-members and filling its archive with documents marked "top secret." Should we see newly communist Romania as a system of nested and competing secret societies? Party leaders and Securitate together form one loose secret society, superordinate to the "masses" whom they exclude through secrecy rules, while the Securitate itself forms another and much more rigorously organized secret society separate from that of the Party. The NKVD/KGB— coming from its own history as a secret society in a time of endemic warfare—needed to protect its new creation from Romania's unreliable Party leadership: strict secrecy and loyalty oaths would encourage that. Only later, as the Securitate and the Romanian Communist Party gradually increased their independence of the Soviet Union, would it be less necessary for the Securitate to operate as a hermetically sealed secret society. But perhaps by then its secret knowledge and practices protected its power position and autonomy from the Party, while helping it penetrate other quasi-secret groups such as dissidents and religious or ethnic minorities.

Because the membership of a secret society is based on prior networks, cleavages in those networks set limits for the structure of the secret society; the cleavages do not have to be extreme in order to have an effect.[81] The networks that nourished the Securitate had come disproportionately from the pre-war secret services, which the NKVD had heavily infiltrated. It was perhaps natural, then, that they should participate in a secret society different from that of other Party members. Finally, if we return to Murphy's vision of secret societies as means of accumulating power and authority by creating dependent clients, we might see the Securitate's secret society as a form of clientelism, which insulated superior officer-patrons' control over their lower-level clients from those of other would-be patrons in the Party hierarchy. Initially, secrecy would have insulated the NKVD/KGB and the Securitate from the Communist Party; later it would insulate the Securitate from the Party and the KGB.

Given the conflicts among the organization's branches and the practices of conspirativity, which meant that many officers would not know who else was in their secret society, we should probably see the Securitate as not one but several secret societies, joined at the top. Various branches were divided into pro-Soviet and pro-American factions, for instance, and as mentioned in the Introduction, the Foreign Intelligence Service (DIE) held itself superior to the other divisions; it was less likely to be in solidary relations with them. Thus, our image of 1950s Romania should be of multiple secret subsocieties, loosely yoked together by their shared sense of mission to protect Romania from its supposed enemies and by their observance of the secrets enabling them to do so. This landscape of secret organizations (including the RCP) related to one another rather like the segments of an-thropology's celebrated segmentary lineage systems, now combined in solidarity against some larger ene-my, now quarreling with one another.

I might summarize what this excursion into the an-thropology of secrecy has contributed so far to think-ing about the Securitate. First, it has suggested the idea that secrecy in the form of conspirativity promot-ed inequality in the organization, as it does in other ethnographic examples, and was thus particularly ad-vantageous to senior officers, supporting their patron-age position as well. Second, it has opened up the rit-ual aspects of recruiting both officers and informers, indicating ways in which their life in the organization became meaningful through the creation of an excit-ing parallel world. Third, it has raised questions found nowhere in scholarship on the secret police, concern-ing the conditions under which secret organizations flourish. This has led us to posit an ecology of compet-ing secret organizations in Romania, as well as multi-ple grounds for claiming patronage, which the secret society helps to insulate from competition. It has also encouraged us to include in our inquiry the epoch-al shifts in gender and class that would have affected male identities at the time of the communist takeover, as did similar shifts in nineteenth-century New York.

115

Equally useful, however, is the opposite procedure: what do we learn from the *differences* between those societies and the secret police? What questions do those differences make us consider? Anikó Szűcs, who has been researching Hungary's ÁVO/ÁVH, asks, What about the idea of a *failed* secret society?[82] What happens when its members turn against and stop trusting each other? How do secret societies fall apart? Perhaps this is an unanticipated way of getting into what happened in Romania in the 1980s: the Securitate's secret society failed as fissures within it widened, some factions joining with factions in the army and Party that had settled upon a change of leadership. The result was Ceauşescu's overthrow in December 1989. And this might be partly a consequence of another peculiarity of the Securitate as a secret society: although the normal situation for secret societies is that their members are visible to one another but not to outsiders, here many members were invisible even to one another, owing to the demands of conspirativity. Can we speak of a secret society when many of its members did not know each other? The organization nonetheless functioned in relative solidarity for several decades. Does this mean that conspirativity rules were honored more in the breach than in the observance? There is some evidence for that possibility. It is obvious, for instance, that several officers engaged in following a target will have to know each other in order to do their job, even if they are unknown to other officers. An article in *Vitralii*, a publication of Securitate veterans, makes this very clear, as the author describes how several agents passed the target off to one another like players in a soccer game.[83] I will consider other evidence for breaches of conspirativity below. In brief, then, in this secret society there were pressures for members to know one another, as they do in most other cases.

A third question concerns what the membership of this secret society consists of: Is it primarily the officers, or should it include the informers as well? In most secret societies, people are either outside the organization or initiated into it, even if through lengthy apprenticeship. In this one, most informers remained attached to the organization in a permanently subordinate status. In discussing initiation I indicated very different scenarios for the recruitment and training of officers and informers. Nonetheless, we know that sometimes people recruited as informers became officers, so where is the line? Moreover, does it matter that many informers *did not want* to be initiated into secrecy and, unlike the officers, were *forced* to join? Does it make sense, then, to treat informers together with the officers, or should we include in the secret society only informers who collaborated willingly? Where do we draw the boundary around this secret society, and what are the effects of having tiers of membership?

Finally, in treating the Securitate as parallel with men's secret cults, I have left out the few women who served as both officers and informers. How does bringing them in make us think differently about the Securitate as a secret society? For example, women's presence might compromise male solidarity—or might be *thought* to do so, owing to gender stereotypes that saw women's primary allegiance as to family and children, not to the organization. Moreover, gender norms interfered with their job performance. One ex-officer interviewed by the CNSAS observed that although women could be hired and indeed were usually more conscientious than the men, "There are certain sensitive things about the work.... A woman can't just go and sit alone in a restaurant! People will talk. For me as a man to go somewhere and get drunk, no problem. But for a woman it's more like, 'Uh, what's she here for, maybe she's trying to pick someone up.' It's tricky."[84] As a result, women were more likely to be employed in office work as secretaries, typists, or archivists than as field operatives. This inhibited their promotion up the hierarchy, however, and would reduce their access to the secrets of the trade—thus reinforcing the Securitate's character as a largely male secret society. All these observations encourage us to return to the anthropology of secrecy with new questions about hierarchies of insiders, rare in that literature.

The Lives of Agents

In the very popular film "The Lives of Others," West German director Florian Henckel von Donnersmarck imagines Stasi captain Gerd Wiesler as a profoundly lonely man except for his vicarious participation in the lives of others, his targets. East Germans criticized the film for making him a sympathetic character who develops a protective attachment to two of them—quite unlikely—, but the image it presented of a solitary person living in an apartment building with other Stasi officers (and sharing the same whore with them) seems plausible. How about the lives of Securitate agents? Is there any way we can glimpse them, amid all the secrecy by which they were bound? One possibility is through officers' personnel files, of which a small number are available to researchers in the CNSAS archive.

I briefly consulted the file of officer Iosif Grigorie Pall, based in Hunedoara county.[85] Included in it are such things as his autobiography, his education and family background, the oaths he has sworn, a list of all the positions he held in the Securitate, as well as his salary, bonuses, promotion details, periodic performance and medical reviews, and testimonials from co-workers. Officer Pall, an ethnic Hungarian from a very modest proletarian family, was recruited in 1953 from his factory job. Having had several years of professional-school training as an electrician, he obtained his high school diploma and law degree through correspondence courses over the next two decades. From his initial rank as a sub-lieutenant, he was promoted to captain in 1962, major in 1968, and lieutenant colonel in 1974, the rank at which he remained until his retirement in April 1989. He and his wife had a son and a daughter, both of whom went to university. Nearly all of his and his wife's relatives were also Hungarian, and they had no relatives abroad. But they did have problems with their kin, for during the war his wife's maternal grandfather had been a member of the "German Ethnic Group," a hitlerite organization of Romania's ethnic-German citizens; for this, Pall was investigated in 1961. He was allowed to keep his post but was told to break off his relations with these kin, which he later said he had done. His file notes that his wife, who worked for a planning institute, had no close friendships but only businesslike relations at work; she had a good friend in her apartment complex, and the couple was visited by unknown persons from other residences. It seems unlikely that their social life was active, for his file states that he often worked late hours.

Officer Pall's career began rather erratically. His performance reviews in the mid-1950s mention his good organizational capacities but criticize him for laxity in his work, his tendency to procrastinate, and his habit of strolling about town during work hours. One superior, criticizing him for timidity, sees it as keeping him from fulfilling his responsibilities. In 1957 he was sanctioned with five days' confinement to his garrison for poor work habits with informers and for not sticking to his established work program. The officer who was to accompany him to an informer meeting found him instead at the house of his girlfriend (who had accompanied him on his strolls through town; he married her that same year).

After this, officer Pall's record gradually began to improve. He is commended for a number of skills: he is an excellent shot, knows how to drive and type, is good at orienting himself in space, excellent at operating eavesdropping devices, and very perspicacious in all he undertakes. Moreover, he is intelligent, with great powers for analyzing and synthesizing informers' reports. Aside from the defect of a quick temper, he has an open and approachable na-

121

ture; displays initiative, honesty, and respectfulness in his relations with superiors; and is irreproachable in his duties as employee, citizen, and family man. His performance review for 1974, when he received his final promotion, is especially laudatory, presenting him as persistent and articulate, with a highly developed capacity for observation and a strong desire to do his job well; good in his work with informers; and superior at resolving both theoretical and practical problems efficiently. The picture becomes even more appealing when we learn that he is very sociable, consumes too many calories (he is judged to be 18 percent overweight), and is a regular drinker of wine, perhaps thereby contributing to his chronic gastroduodenitis.

The overall impression that emerges from this brief file (about two hundred pages covering over thirty years) is of a rather lackluster young man whom the Securitate has whipped into shape, making him an example of extensive upward mobility. He develops a capacity to nurture his fellow officers and subordinates, and he focuses his considerable talents. The categories in terms of which he is assessed reveal the organization's priorities, including a preoccupation with his character and his kinship and social networks. In my personal experience of him, Lt. Col. Pall was indeed conscientious and perspicacious, directing his informers to keep me under close watch and analyzing the results intelligently. He distinguishes himself among my case officers by being the only one to determine that I was *not* a spy.[86] I like to think that he received his promotion in 1974 on my account: his performance review for 1973-74 has him covering counterespionage by US and UK "tourists" in the exact area where I was living. He recruited new informers there, undertaking some "special actions" relevant to counterespionage and "successfully preventing the flow of state secrets."[87]

Since retired officer Pall and the other *Securiști* I approached in 2011 and 2012 declined to be interviewed and the published sources I have read are silent on this point, I can say little more about secrecy as a way of life for *Securiști*. What were its effects on their relationship to the organization and to other people? Did conspirativity atomize them? Lacking firm answers for the Securitate, I turn for inspiration to Andreas Glaeser's interviews with twenty-five Stasi officers in his book *Political Epistemics*, which I will supplement with anecdotal evidence from Romania.[88] Owing to the systems for housing distribution and allocation of vacation spots, he found, Stasi officers tended to live in the same buildings and neighborhoods as other Stasi officers, to send their children to the same schools, and to spend their vacations in the

123

company of other Stasi officers and military personnel. They were all expected to support the sports club "Dynamo," operated by the Interior Ministry. Thus, workplace relations heavily determined the home environment.[89]

Glaeser found among the officers he interviewed a strong sense of identification with the organization and its goals and a deep sense of patriotism—likely true of the Securitate as well. Describing how Stasi officers' sense of belonging came in part from their patterns of association, narrowly focused on other Stasi employees, he writes:

Long daily and weekly work hours increased on the one hand their absolute face time with "comrades of mind" (*Gesinnungsgenossen*). On the other hand, it limited their opportunities to maintain sustained contact with others.... [R]elationships [with people critical of the Party] could now create problems for the officers as the Stasi almost jealously guarded their contacts with the outside world. The strict rules of secrecy were a structural impediment to the building or maintenance of [outside relationships]. The officers took these rules very seriously as they saw them to be constitutive of their work and their identities.... They prevented them from sharing much about their everyday lives in the Stasi, and certainly nothing about the material core of their work, that is the operative tasks they were involved in.[90]

Concerning family life, Glaeser writes: "The rules of secrecy were already a potential strain on their relations with their wives and children, as conversations remained strangely asymmetrical. While family members were supposed to share their lives outside of the house, the officers remained largely mute. That some wives felt 'locked out' of the work life of their husbands was underscored by some wives' interest in my interviews with their officer husbands. Friends, too, had to be tolerant of such restrictions, respect for which was much more likely among other functionaries dedicated to the party-state."[91] Gusterson, likewise, sees practices of secrecy at the weapons laboratory he studied as socially isolating, "a means of creating a disciplinary distance between weapons scientists and their families."[92]

I interviewed a woman friendly with a *Securist*'s wife, who would periodically say to her, "Never marry one. You never know when he's coming home, you don't know where he's going, you don't know who he is, or even what his name is. If he gets very upset with you and grabs your arm, he'll dislocate your shoulder because he's in such good physical condition. And they have no feelings at all." To my questions about the social lives of agents, a CNSAS employee intimately familiar with the archive answered by saying that the image of these workers was of "heroic, frustrated, not-family-oriented people. They didn't go from home to their job: they were on the job all the time." From an associate who had worked for many years teaching Securitate officers, I learned that he had not one friend from work, claiming he had no time for it. He socialized seldom, mainly with relatives. His wife later echoed this: "Colleagues—you'd think there'd be relations with colleagues, but I don't know a single one of his, and because of him I couldn't develop friendships either. If he died tomorrow, I'd have no one to call to the funeral." Victor Mitran provides some data about the work that kept officers away from home. Those engaged in shadowing a target had to write a report at the end of each day, detailing all the target's movements; writing the report could take several hours and might keep the officer at his desk well past midnight.[93] According to Oprea, socializing was reduced not only because of work hours but because if one met with people other than those from the Ministry of the Interior, one would have to report it.[94] Perhaps these habits and personal characteristics contributed to the rumored 30 percent divorce rate of Securitate officers following the 1989 revolution.[95]

The manipulation of family ties—both among the

general populace and among their own—was characteristic of the Stasi, Securitate, and other East European secret police. The Stasi sought to influence officers' choice of partner, reserving until the very end of the regime the right to reject their employees' proposed spouses. Glaeser quotes a speech given by a Stasi official in 1985: "'There are more and more examples where young comrades no longer take a partisan position in choosing their life partners. They increasingly decide for the partner and against our organ ... *the dismissals for this reason prove this point.*'"[96] In Hungary, if an officer wanted to get married, the firm conducted "a detailed environmental study" of the proposed partner.[97] A CNSAS employee replied to my question about similar Securitate constraints on marriage by saying, "It wasn't written out in black and white, but a lot of pressure was put on people." Former Securitate officer Constantin Bucur noted the same thing: "When I was in training, I had a colleague they expelled after two years because he married the daughter of a priest. I had a girlfriend whose family had been Greek partisans, and the school commander said to me, 'Either school or your girlfriend.' It wasn't honorable what I did, but I chose school."[98] Bucur had reason to know about the Securitate's policy on kinship: he eventually had to leave the organization, he said, for having a brother-in-law who collaborated actively with Radio Free Europe. Supporting all these impressions are the main characters of Coruț's novel *Quinta spartă:* an elderly intelligence officer known only as "the old man," "a man without a real name, without a family, and without an address," and a younger one who lacks a wife, children, and even a dwelling.[99]

Learning that in the late 1980s over 90 percent of new recruits to the Stasi were coming from Stasi families, Glaeser concludes that the organization was on its way to becoming a caste.[100] Transmission of Securitate employment is anecdotally reported for Romania as well. One woman I spoke with had met a young man in the 1980s who, when she asked him his life plans, replied that he wanted to be a Securitate officer because his uncle was one, lived very well, and had promised to help him get in. An employee of the CNSAS with whom I discussed the question said there was considerable cross-generational inheritance of Securitate work and described how male officers would try to get good office jobs for their daughters, so they wouldn't have to work as hard. In his CNSAS interview, ex-officer Gheorghe Țârlescu claimed to know of many officers whose children had joined the post-1989 secret service and were being guided by their parents in learning the trade.[101] Finally, a university professor I spoke with had had a student who translated Securitate manuals into Arabic for its Palestinian training school; the student's father was also a Securitate employee. When I commented on this inheritance of Securitate work, she replied, "Those were the only people they could trust."

Although many patterns characteristic of the Stasi seem to obtain for the Securitate as well, it is important to note the possible effects of differences in the size of the officer corps. Whereas the Stasi had a total of 93,000 officers for a population of 17 million, Romania had only 39,000 for a population of 23 million. This means that Securitate officers were spread much more thinly across the landscape. In consequence they might be more likely to associate with employees in other branches of the Ministry of the Interior (such as the police) or in the state administration, rather than primarily among themselves. Inheritance of Securitate status was probably also less frequent than for the Stasi, where the 1960s and late 1970s brought no significant ruptures in policy, as occurred in Romania.

The observance of secrets continues today, as most ex-Securitate officers refuse to speak outside their circle. I learned from an ethnographer involved in excavating cadavers of persons killed in the 1950s that officers will not talk about the events surrounding those deaths: to his questions, they reply only, "I don't know

129

anything." Not even government prosecutors can get them to talk.[102] In the personnel file of officer Iosif Pall are his retirement papers from April 1989, which include his sworn oath not to reveal any of the secrets of his work.[103] The main exception to the rule of silence is the handful of officers who have written memoirs, most of whom felt in some way wronged by the organization (they were pensioned early for being on the losing side of an internal conflict, for instance, or for having relatives who collaborated with Radio Free Europe). We are left with many unanswered questions concerning the lives of agents.

Secrecy and Socialism

So far I have been locating secrecy primarily in a set of organizations—the Communist Party, the Securitate, the KGB—and focusing on its social-structural entailments. Over time, however, secrecy gradually infiltrated Romania more and more. In 1971 the new Law on the Defense of the State Secret made the entire society responsible for protecting secrets.[104] In this way the secrecy first dictated by persecution of the Bolsheviks under the Tsar's secret police gradually expanded to take over the life of all Romanians. The change had partly to do with changes in the Party's leadership style after the mid-1960s, following its full consolidation of control over the country as well as Ceauşescu's securing his power as General Secretary. These involved a broader "massification" of the Party and new forms of governmentality, as violence diminished in favor of softer methods of surveillance: now *everybody* was supposed to keep and discover secrets, making vigilance a constant frame of mind and emergent aspect of subjectivities. The population as a whole would become its own surveillance instrument, and the domain of the secret would become boundless.

That expansion reminds us that the content of the secrets is often less significant than the practices to which they are subjected. The new law would not change the content of "the state secret" but required internalizing and enforcing new practices around it. Moving to consider secrecy as a technology or set of practices that had certain specificities in socialism, I will once more take my examples from conspirativity. I will comment on a few of its unintended consequences, then return to the conundrum I mentioned at the start of the chapter: how we can square the Securitate's reputation for fearsomeness with its sometimes-absurd inner workings. I end with some observations about the "state effect" of secrecy in socialism's legitimation.

131

Secrecy as technology and practices

At the level of content—the thing that is hidden (people's "real" identities as spies or enemies, the specific practices of surveillance the Securitate employs, and so forth)—secrecy is based upon a negation of speech or an injunction to silence concerning some specific information. Unlike silence, however, which can result not from suppressed speech but from simply having nothing to say, secrecy always involves a willed suppression. As such, it also always involves the possibility of discovery. According to Lochrie, all the major theorists of secrecy refer to its basic paradox: "that it implies its own exposure, that it limns the explicit statement and the body of knowledge..."[105] When we focus on secrecy as concealment of content, then, it automatically implies *revelation, or disclosure*, and the practices by which this occurs.

Michael Taussig helps us take this point further. He writes, "The power of negation built into the secrecy depends upon the fearsome expectation of its transgression as indicated by the threatened penalties.... [T]he secret (and hence the transgression that has to break through it) has in fact *to be not only concealed but revealed as well*."[106] Taussig understands this back-and-forth movement between concealment and revelation, with each revelation evoking further concealment and so on, as generating a "fund of power." The dialectic of concealment and revelation can take place at any level—between informers and officers, as I will describe in the next chapter, or on up the hierarchy.

In socialism, that dialectic took on a characteristic form, especially in the early years, in practices of *unmasking and denunciation*. They could occur at any time and involve people of all social categories, and they were especially crucial in building the center's "fund of power" through the purges by which newly established communist parties consolidated their regimes. It was the secret police who had the job of creating and verifying the secret truths that would get a rival eliminated, perhaps executed. That these truths might as easily be fabrications gives the concealment-revelation cycle a new twist: what was concealed could well be that the revealed secret was a lie.[107] No matter: the movement between a secret and its disclosure was inscribed at the heart of these power struggles, and the secret police was its executor.[108] The expulsion of people from the leadership through show trials based on the revelation of secrets once again underscores the importance of seeing secrecy in terms of practices of concealment, rather than primarily as a matter of the actual information that was often their pretext. The revelation might be strictly performative: Belu Zilber

133

recalls in his memoir a meeting with an interrogator, who puts two thick files on the table before him but never opens them. What is revealed is the fact that he controls volumes of information, not what that information is.[109] Similarly, Vatulescu writes of the "spectacle of secrecy," in which "files were routinely paraded in front of the public"; she gives the example of a documentary film in which the viewer could see the writing on the files but not read the actual words.[110]

Importantly, in his discussion Taussig also draws our attention to the total social field containing the movement between concealment and disclosure, and specifically to the role of those most fully excluded from the secrets (he is talking of initiation rites, where the excluded are usually women). These outsiders, he says, engage in an "active unknowing" of what is going on with the secrets of initiation, an active unknowing that is itself "a subtle expression of revelation and concealment, for the women know they must not know but in fact do 'know' a good deal." In other words, the effects of concealing secrets from the outside and revealing them within depend on a "larger scheme of revelation in that the secrecy at issue is strategically incomplete, being an open or public secret to some extent shared by all."[111] Taussig is cautioning us that those whom a secret excludes, within the wider social structure that secrecy has cleft in twain, nonetheless have an idea of what it is about, and this shapes their behavior as social beings.

Moreover, it has significant consequences: the efficacy of the Securitate as the ultimate organ of social control and generator of fear comes precisely from the "open secret" that a secret police exists and is constantly uncovering or fabricating secrets and recruiting informers. Let me briefly illustrate Taussig's point from a conversation I had with my friend Mariana, whom I met in the early 1980s. In 1988 Mariana confessed to me that she had been filing informers' reports on me for several years but was no longer doing so. Like Nicolae Corbeanu, whose case I mentioned at the start of the chapter, she noticed no consequences of her decision to stop informing.[112] As she told me in 2010 when we discussed it once more, that decision did not improve her relations with her other friends, though, whom she had never told about her informing because she had sworn never to divulge it—and she felt guilty toward them on that account. Even after she stopped informing, then, she was caught in a web of secrecy that was both the Securitate's and her own. Although she herself knew the secret of her recruitment—and that it was possible to break free—she still felt bound by her secrecy oath. Because she would not tell her friends that they too could refuse to collaborate and suffer no consequences, they all remained terrified of the possibility of being approached for recruitment, about which they "knew" without having been initiated themselves. Their active unknowing helped to make the Securitate seemingly omnipotent and ubiquitous—crucial to its instilling and maintaining fear.

There were a number of practices entailed in keeping some things hidden while revealing others. We are already familiar with several of them: practices of knowledge transmission, initiation rituals, loyalty oaths, code names, secrecy designations for documents (top secret, and so on), and, the most far-reaching, conspirativity. All are *technologies of exclusion*, drawing a boundary (or a series of boundaries) between those who "know something" and those who do not, or who know less. In the previous section I described the field of power within which the secret as a technology first took on its socialist form: a landscape pulsating with different organizations or subgroups within them, engaged in continual struggles for supremacy. In this context, secrecy was the most potent technology of exclusion, setting hard boundaries to assist its practitioners in maintaining their position in the competitive environment. Even though secrecy was official practice in many areas of Romanian society, the Securitate was the institution that had come to monopolize these techniques most successfully. (Might it be that the 1971 law on the state secret, by making "the entire people" the guarantor of secrecy, intentionally infringed on the Securitate's monopoly of this exclusionary technique?)

From among secrecy's practices, let us look more closely at conspirativity as a technology of exclusion. "The purpose of secrecy," wrote Simmel, "is, above all, protection ... Of all protective measures, the most radical is to make oneself invisible."[113] Through practices of conspirativity that helped make them invisible, the Securitate as a whole and its sub-branches protected its power position with unusual thoroughness—against the citizenry, the KGB, and to a considerable extent against the Romanian Communist Party. Conspirativity (note the common root with "conspiracy") began as a way of protecting communist militants and then became crucial to protecting informers' and officers' cover—a function for which it is used among intelligence services more widely. It helped to ensure sources of information: a work plan from the late 1970s states, "The principle of collaboration of the Securitate organs with working people implicitly presupposes respect for the principle of conspirativity, precisely so their fundamental rights can be fully protected.... Citizens who assist the Securitate organs [i.e., informers] must be convinced that all measures will be taken to preserve the discretion

137

necessary to their contribution."[114] Besides protecting their anonymity, the practice had the additional benefit of preventing informers from developing any form of solidarity among themselves and breaking free of their handlers, since none of them knew who any of the others were. Conspirativity was also crucial to officers' flexibility in working with informers, enabling them to use completely different tactics with each one without fear of comparison.

But secrecy in practice also had a number of drawbacks. I already observed that for members of the organization, conspirativity was socially isolating and created problems with officers' family relations. For the Stasi, Glaeser writes that the pressures on Stasi officers concerning upward reporting of information tended to prevent integrative interpretations and analysis, partly because, "it was always argued that those higher up knew more because they received more information from more sides and thus were assumed to be much better able to synthesize data and then to draw the necessary conclusions."[115] He continues, "The range of problems Stasi officers tried to fix is astonishing even if they ultimately had to concede, with regret, that the means available to them as secret police were insufficient to tackle any of them. They tried to fix supply problems by short-circuiting information flows otherwise blocked by red tape. And yet they could do so only to a moderate degree since their own internal secrecy requirements limited the flow of information."[116] In an indictment of the effects of conspirativity, Glaeser concludes that the rules of secrecy so isolated Stasi officers as to hinder their success in dealing with the dissidents they were supposed to be containing.[117]

Hungarian scholars Tabajdi and Ungváry offer a wonderful instance of the pitfalls of conspirativity. The "Sole Mio" was an elite Budapest bar and hotel intended for Western Europeans, set up by state security with built-in bugs, wiretaps, and cameras in both the bar and the hotel rooms. To found such an establishment, however, required the close collaboration of several state organizations, including the Hungarian Collectives' Association, the Budapest Council, the Beverage Distribution Collective, and the III/I Department of the Ministry of Interior. The collaboration proved impossible in the long term, for a variety of reasons. Only a few weeks after it opened in 1969, the half-finished, underequipped and under-attended bar was forced to close: it had been deconspired by one of the venture's many partners, who gradually realized why he had been told to order special bar tables.[118]

We have several examples of how conspirativity might have impeded work performance for the Securitate. Consider the effects of the following injunction.

139

For reasons of "counterinformational protection" (that is, conspirativity), no worker—not even the most experienced—was permitted to search the organization's entire database of names; instead, the names were divided alphabetically, with any given officer responsible for only one, two, or at most three letters.[119] This practice would make it nearly impossible for anyone to use the data base efficiently. In addition, conspirativity impeded communicating well within the organization by reducing officers' ability to discuss the particulars of cases, as is suggested by an article in *Securitatea* magazine: "In meetings by section and by unit—and this includes Party meetings as well—we aim not to reveal (*deconspira*) problems, cases, concrete methods but to discuss only in general terms, without giving names or localities."[120] Further insight comes from an interview with former Securitate officer Gheorghe Țârlescu, in the CNSAS Oral History Archive. Among other things, Țârlescu describes the enormous amount of time he wasted trying to recruit as an informer a long-time acquaintance, whom conspirativity prevented from revealing that he was already working for a different officer. The interviewer then says, "Your colleagues didn't know who was working with whom," to which he replies, "*Theoretically speaking*, no, but in *practice*.... There was compartmentalization, fine, but people didn't respect it, because after all, *you're working in the same space.* One guy goes on vacation and someone has to take over his work…"[121] With this, the contradiction—so common in ethnography—between rules and their practices comes clearly into view.

Secrecy as obstruction

These observations lead us to consider a different aspect of secrecy as practice. Writing about the vast increase in the classification of documents as "secret" in the US since September 11, 2001, Peter Galison writes, "Suppose we ask about the transmission of knowledge not by asking the usual social studies of knowledge question, How does replication occur? but instead by probing the staggeringly large effort devoted to *impeding* the transmission of knowledge."[122] A society like Romania's under Ceaușescu fits that description beautifully. Indeed, I think it is appropriate to see secrecy as participating in a larger set of *technologies of obstruction*, with practices that obstruct the flow of information even as they seek to gather it. I sometimes think, in my ideal-type moments, of the "motors" of socialism and capitalism as differing on the dimension of *flow*. Capital accumulation thrives on the turnover of capital, on its increasing veloci-

141

ty, on speeding up the process of making and selling goods and services, on ever-greater sophistication in convincing people to consume so as to increase the turnover time of capital, on reducing the "friction of distance," on the ready availability of endless supplies of credit, and so forth. It immobilizes capital in the form of fixed capital only so as to increase flows further. The epitome of this trend is the replacement of transmission cables in 2013 so as to increase the speed of stock-market trades by billionths of a second.

Socialism, not having capital accumulation as its main goal, did not place the same premium on flow. The way things worked out within the constraints of central planning was rather the opposite: "supply-constrained" economies, or economies of shortage, which are exactly about the lack of flow in socialism. Hoarding, that hallmark of socialist production; CMEA export controls, that hallmark of socialist trade; censorship, that hallmark of socialist publishing (and communication more generally); and so on—all were means of obstructing flows, and secrecy was another. It obstructed the flow of information both outward and within. In doing so, it served tendencies important to the leadership: deterring the accumulation of knowledge in alternative centers of power not under the Party's control (I invoke here Jan Gross's argument about socialism's "spoiler state"),[123] and reducing the availability of information that might promote resistance or keep people from developing the desired socialist consciousness.

To think further about how secrecy obstructed flows, I invoke Foucault's celebrated piece "What Is an Author?," in which he suggests that an author (or what he calls the "author function") is "the principle of thrift in the proliferation of meaning."[124] It helps to keep the abundance of signification in check by gathering meanings together under names, which in capitalist societies then enter into systems of property rights. In a sense, secrecy is like authorship: a principle of thrift, a bounding and sorting mechanism with respect to the use of information, parallel in some respects to putting property rights on signification but in a different, less "capitalist," idiom. Secrecy bounds communities and sorts people into those who are allowed or not allowed to "profit" from knowledge and information. "Top secret" and other designations are always relative to a community (the Securitate, certain groups within it, the Communist Party, the "entire people," and so on.). Some such principle of thrift is necessary for a profession—intelligence-gathering— that uses a very broad definition of "information." Like ethnographers, *Securişti* think that potentially *everything* is information; *any* detail might possibly reveal an enemy behind the mask of an ally and thereby

143

serve the Securitate's purifying function. To manage such abundance, secrecy is an aid. Beyond the work of intelligence, though, obstructing the flow of information through secrecy is critical to the Party's broader goal of transforming consciousness, channeling thought in "correct" directions, cutting down alternative formulations. Expanding the reach of secrecy—fetishizing technologies of concealment and obstruction—contributes to that goal.

As I have been showing, however, the demands of maintaining secrecy produced work practices that complicated it. Chief among them was conspirativity, with its left-hand-doesn't-know-what-the-right-hand-is-doing outcomes, its duplication of effort, and its propagation of "authors" (people following targets, people censoring correspondence, people installing microphones, people listening to them and transcribing, people giving reports, people writing up those reports, people reading and commenting on the results of all this work). Within the institution, conspirativity generated loquacity, redundancy, rather than thrift—a tendency furthered by the creeping effects of the Law on the Defense of the State Secret, as Király has analyzed it (above). Even without conspirativity there was redundancy, for as Horváth and Szakolczai demonstrated, there were parallel information-gathering processes going on, as not only the secret police but also Communist Party instructors spent tremendous amounts of time gathering information.[125] The main difference is that the Securitate specialized in doing so *under the constraints of secrecy*, which insulated its information from that of parallel efforts. Secrecy as method and practice set it off, perhaps enabling it to claim that its information was better.[126]

The obstructions of secrecy produced other problems too, paralleling those in the larger society. In all socialist societies, attempts at obstruction called forth remedies. The constraints of the "first economy" called forth various bargaining and procurement strategies, as well as encouraging the second economy, to keep production from freezing up altogether.[127] Censorship called forth samizdat. Information hoarding called forth wildly proliferating rumor (some of it no doubt planted by the Securitate itself). And secrecy? Might it have called forth information sharing and other breaches? Reporting on a very different secret society, Gusterson writes of the California nuclear weapons scientists he studied, who were also governed by the rule of secrecy: "The Laboratory's system of secrecy appears more seamless and totalizing in theory, when stated as a set of rules, than in practice, when the rules may be enforced ambiguously and complied with erratically."[128] He quotes an employee who said, "'The "need to know" doctrine underlying the secrecy was regularly compromised by people using information to trade for information.'"[129] Given what we know about the high levels of personalism in the socialist system, it is hard to believe that anyone could keep all the secrets they were supposed to. One can imagine informers boasting about their connection to an important *Securist*; alternatively, we read about people recruited as informers who then, in violation of their secrecy oath, told others about it, thereby rendering themselves useless to their handlers. Here is one such example, from the memoirs of a person approached as an informer: "I knew them to be capable of great harm. So in that same sleepless night I formulated my tactics: to tell the Securitate's proposal all over the place, in such a way that it would reach their ears. To make myself unusable by them."[130]

Cosma singles out the Foreign Intelligence Service (DIE) as an egregious violator of secrecy rules. As I mentioned earlier, DIE officers tended to be better educated, better paid—in a word, classier—and to consider themselves an elite within the organization. "In that unit, the atmosphere of idle chit-chat and boastfulness allowed some cadres to find out data and secret information from other work compartments…. [The DIE leadership] treated with condemnable lightness the vital problems of defending the secrets of work and the need for conspirativity around some actions"; one result was chaos in the unit's organization and daily activity.[131] Troncotă offers another nice example involving the same unit. Commenting on the division and increasingly tense relations between it and other divisions of the Securitate after the early 1960s, which sometimes involved "unfair competition," he writes, "Every county Securitate branch had a bureau represented by one or two DIE officers. These people, in exchange for certain small presents (coffee, cigarettes, soaps, fine drink) obtained from abroad by courier by their colleagues at the center, succeeded in effectively 'stealing' important information, that is, they appropriated for themselves with minimum effort the work of the officers from internal counterespionage and military counterinformation."[132] Such information-sharing was not strictly speaking an infringement of secrecy rules, since it was occurring within the organization rather than across its boundaries, but it alerts one to the possibility of comparable "leaks" elsewhere. This is in any case the impression one gets from reading, for instance, a 1984 secret memo that tightened the circuit of information to prevent violations of conspirativity.[133] One reason, we might suspect, was that it was impossible to work effectively within its constraints.

Another reason might have been the near-total impaction brought about by the ever-proliferating defense of the state secret. Király summarizes thus the relation between the secret and socialism as of the 1980s: "a totally intertwined dispersal and confusion, which no one any longer reins in nor could they, rendering useless all the desperate coercive efforts ... to maintain control over it. Spy-mania, nebulous and paroxysmal visions of conspiracies the whole universe was planning with tireless diligence against 'the country' and 'the people' are nothing more, however, than the natural manner in which the [one who institutes secrets] himself views the world."[134] In those same years my file reveals me as the object of exactly that vision.

The State Effect

"It is on the basis of secrecy," Nugent writes, "that states work their magic."[135] This leads me to conclude my ethnography of Securitate secrecy with some thoughts on what Timothy Mitchell, building on Foucault and Philip Abrams, has called "the state effect." Mitchell writes, "[T]he phenomenon we name 'the state' arises from techniques that enable mundane material practices to take on the appearance of an abstract, non-material form"—an appearance that nonetheless has concrete practical consequences.[136] Essential to this state effect in Romania was secrecy, providing part of the "magic" that made the Romanian Party-state appear to stand as an integrated entity above and outside "the entire people."[137] Contrary to the perceptions of its citizens, that entity was not a coherent, unified actor. Despite the centralizing efforts of Party leaders Gheorghiu-Dej and Ceaușescu, the field of power at the center was highly fragmented among disparate competing groups—a secret amply revealed by the chaos after Ceaușescu's fall. If that inner chaos was not apparent to most Romanians, the "mask" of secrecy—its state effect— was one reason.

An important ingredient in that outcome was, of course, fear, the emotion the Securitate had primary responsibility for maintaining among the citizenry. In the division of labor among organs of the state, the Securitate held the keys to the kingdom of fear. Fear was partly an effect of secrecy: most people were afraid of the Securitate even though they did not know how it really worked, aside from rumors of brutality and torture in the 1950s and '60s that had caused outright terror. As I indicated in my account of my friend Mariana's untransgressed secrecy oath, not even the significant reduction in violent methods after 1965 did away with people's fear, though their terror may have diminished. Even so, the effects of fear in those days could last a lifetime, as we see from the comment of a peasant interviewed by Oprea in 2011 who said,

"Even now when I hear a car engine I'm afraid, because the Secu used to be the only ones with cars."[138] Years of urinating in his pants at the sound of an automobile had marked him permanently.

Fear was also an effect of the *invisibility* that secrecy enabled. The Securitate's invisibility made it seem omnipresent; like Czechoslovakia's StB, described by Williams and Deletant, it "relied not on random terror, but on a reputation for prevalence,"[139] carefully cultivated. One never knew when and how it would enter one's life, with potentially devastating consequences. Király asks, Whence the secret's power and intrinsic force?, answering, "this force resides in its wholly peculiar capacity to produce abstractions. Everything that becomes secret loses its 'palpability' and 'visibility,' thus in a way its concreteness."[140] That contributed a thorough-going uncertainty to social life (recall Troncotă's observation that the Securitate was the principal factor that created *in*security[141]). No one was certain who the officers were, who was informing, how much information was being obtained, or how it would be used. I emphasize that the fear was not simply of a repressive power understood as coming "from the top": people knew that potentially *anyone* could be collaborating with the Securitate, creating a pervasive sense of unease. In short, Securitate secrecy was about most people's *not knowing* in some fundamental areas of existence, having no secure categories for organizing experience or planning their lives. That insecurity generated fear. Did such fear help to create and maintain people's belief in the Securitate's omnipresence—help to make it a kind of Ur-secret, like the terrifying monsters of New Guinea secret cults?

As I have indicated above, the tendency over time was for the idiom of secrecy to multiply and expand, becoming the duty of the entire people, the defense of which would ostensibly bind them to their state. In the event, it was primarily the Securitate who were so bound, owing to their deep immersion in the world-making quality of secrecy. Beginning as a protective device in wartime, it then became the grounds for identity and action, providing for its members a language and an entire parallel, make-believe world governed by their own (some would call it paranoid) vision. This vision placed them at the center of the defense of the Romanian nation, which they would protect by finding and expelling enemies, pollutants, sources of contamination. I believe many saw their task as akin to a sacred charge. Julie Fedor writes of the Securitate's ancestor, the Soviet Cheka, which built up a sacred cult, having its own saints, sacred sites, sacraments, aura of mystery, and cosmology sustaining a moral universe whose purity it was their job to uphold.[142] Echoes of these ideas, as I noted above,

151

can be found among Securitate officers as well, in their reputed fascination with the occult and in the spy novels of ex-*Securist* writers such as Pavel Coruț.[143]

Indeed, a connection between the secret and the sacred goes back to Durkheim's *Elementary Forms of the Religious Life*, where he sees the secret as central to organizing the distinction between the sacred and the profane. Likewise Taussig, labeling secrecy and its transgression "a potent stimulus to creativity, to what Simmel called 'the magnification of reality,' by means of the sensation that behind the appearance of things there is a deeper, mysterious, reality, that we may here call the sacred."[144] That connection with mystery undergirds the state effect of the secret in socialism, strengthening Canetti's observation with which I opened my chapter: "Secrecy lies at the very core of power." If, as Mitchell suggests, the state effect of western modernity rests on the "transparency" of the apparent separation of "the political" from both "economy" and "society,"[145] then the state effect of socialism resided in its *opacity*, within which were hidden the terror, the awe, the mystery, and the secrets for which the Securitate was the primary agent.

Has learning of all the ineptitude in the Securitate's practice of secrecy negated this mystique? The empirical answer to that question will have to come from those Romanian citizens who feared it, but in principle I would suspect not. Knowing the mechanics of a theatrical performance does not prevent an audience from being moved, frightened, or unhinged by the experience. We dismiss the effects of Securitate secrecy only if we are tricked by the secret's illusion that what is at issue is its content or its truth. Perhaps this ethnographic attempt to defamiliarize the Securitate as a secret society has helped to broaden our sense of what endows the secret with its intrinsic force.

* * *

According to Michel de Certeau, the "elementary structure" of the secret is that it "localizes the confrontation between a *will to know* and a *will to conceal*."[146] In this chapter I have been at pains to set aside the will to know in favor of exploring the will to conceal, but in my final chapter I take up the other side of the equation. Among secrecy's effects, a number of scholars have noted, are its consequences for ideas about truth. It sets in place a specific conception of truth and knowledge, about which Nadkarni writes, "if secrecy is the very index of truth, then truth by its very nature becomes something that must be secret."[147] This makes revelation the ultimate guarantee of truthfulness. Glaeser continues the point: "[T]ruth now came to be seen as something that will not reveal itself unless it is pursued through the clandestine methods of the secret police."[148] He calls this a "*secret police model of truth*. Truth cannot be seen directly, it must be spied out."[149] That is, as if by a mimetic principle, to find a secret one must be hidden oneself; to seek knowledge requires disguise.

A key instrument of Securitate truth-seeking—and an unusual form of disguise—alongside those other secret means (the letter-censors, the microphones, the hidden cameras) came to be *the informer*. Additional effects of secrecy include the ways it changes both the nature of the social whole in which it is exercised and the people it implicates, as well: "The practice of secrecy transforms scientists by reworking the web of relationships they inhabit and thus their sense of self," says Gusterson.[150] In my final chapter, I will explore these themes: the Securitate's pursuit of knowledge and truth, in particular its use of informers and its reshaping of social networks—and of the people they contained.

Chapter 3

Knowledge Practices and the Social Relations of Surveillance

> Surveillance, then, was not designed to uncover popular sentiments and moods, nor was it intended merely to keep people under control; its whole purpose was to act on people, to change them…. Surveillance was not a passive, observational endeavor; it was an active, constructivist one.
>
> —Peter Holquist, "Information"

On April 1, 1974, Securitate officer Iosif Pall in Deva, Hunedoara county, responded as follows to a communication from Bucharest that I was collecting military information:

From the data our organs hold, two hypotheses can be raised: 1) Katherine Verdery is collecting military information, for which reason she travels in zones where there are special military units, discussing special problems with inhabitants of these zones as well as with workers at the [armaments] factory in Cugir. 2) Katherine Verdery is collecting information limited to the problems of her doc-

155

toral thesis, contacting intellectuals who can give her valid information about customs, local folklore, and problems of anthropology.[1]

He listed a few items in support of the first hypothesis and then proposed a number of concrete steps to clarify the situation. His superiors approved the measures and gave him until May 10 to analyze the results. Following a year's additional verification, however, after I had left Romania Lieutenant Colonel Pall wrote a lengthy report concluding *against* the first hypothesis:

> From the material administered, it does not follow that she carried on any infractional activity against the Romanian Socialist Republic. The relations she created during her stay in Romania do not have suspect character along the lines of counterespionage. We therefore propose closing her file.[2]

A decade later, officers Ioan Oprea, Gheorghe Diaconescu, Ioan Şerbănoiu, and Filitaş Vulcan sent up to Major-General Ştefan Alexie of the Third Directorate in Bucharest the quite different results of their similar investigation in the city of Cluj:

> Report with proposals for concluding the case of "VERA" [later labeled "CIA agent"]. From the com-

plex informative-operative surveillance measures undertaken concerning her, it has resulted that her proposed research is merely a cover for unfolding an intense activity for collecting socio-political information and for studying certain Romanian citizens and attracting them into antisocial activity. "VERA" is preoccupied with obtaining socio-political information that has no connection whatever with her research properly speaking.... After she gathers and verifies the information, she synthesizes it in numbered reports... using a special system of abbreviations and conspiratorial names for her sources,... typed in three copies and sent to the U.S.A. Embassy in Bucharest by special courier.... We note that "VERA" does not keep a single copy, as would be normal if she were using them to write a scientific work.... From photocopies [we made] of her notes it results that the information obtained by "VERA" has a hostile character toward our country, as she constantly seeks to bring out the dissatisfactions and resistant attitudes toward the politics of our Party and state on the part of those whom she exploits for informative purposes. To obtain this information, she made contacts with certain nationalist Hungarian elements, whose hostile attitudes she sought to amplify... [as our organs ascertained] by checking their conversations with recording devices....

157

Bearing in mind that her presence in our country is aimed at collecting tendentious information of a socio-political character and is at the same time of a nature to stimulate the activity of hostile elements, we consider it necessary to put a stop to this activity.[3]

Beyond this (as I noted in my Introduction), they explicitly liken my information-gathering practices to their own, confirming their view that I have experience in espionage. [4]

These reports introduce the theme of the present chapter: the practices whereby the Securitate sought to create knowledge about reality, uncovering the secrets that might prove dangerous to the government. As a member of the larger class of surveillance institutions, the Securitate was a kind of information machine whose job was to serve national security by collecting information and processing it.[5] To do so, like many other producers of or seekers after knowledge, they created hypotheses and developed methods of verification. They spent a great deal of time surveying the landscape, trolling through mountains of data to find things of interest, and looking for patterns. Like all collectors of information, they applied to this process a specific theoretical filter, one arising from the concept of plot or conspiracy, which produced specific kinds of "truth" about dangers to the state. Because

the truth the officers were seeking differed significantly from that of people who have used these files since
1989, their filter makes the archive less useful to us
as a *source* of knowledge than as a *form* of it,[6] whose
practices I will discuss here. These practices afforded
them a significant advantage because given their cer-
tainty that everyone was up to something, their filter
provided them with a tool for discerning it: the notion of networks, the operative unit in a conspiracy.
The aim of their knowledge practices was to discover and then disable the networks that harbored dangers to the regime.

Understanding power as not just a repressive force
but also a productive one intertwined with knowledge,[7] this chapter will explore the process of knowledge production and information gathering by the
Securitate. I will argue that their most important
methods for producing knowledge were at the same
time socially transformative, aiming to produce a new
social landscape, with implications for creating the
"new socialist person" and a new society. I do not claim
that this case is unique: many governments and organizations have engaged in similar transformational
projects and mobilized informers for them, including
not only the early modern police but the mendicant
orders and Protestant consistories, among others. My
goal, rather, is to contribute to better understanding

159

this one, which is now possible for the first time, with the opening of this archive. Once more, I emphasize that my research is still in an early stage.

Before I proceed, I wish to provide brief historical context for this part of my discussion and to justify my view that it makes sense to treat the Securitate as knowledge practitioners. First, as occurred in all East European countries, Romania's secret police engaged in countless acts of brutality from the late 1940s up through the early 1960s. People were beaten and killed with abandon, exiled to hard labor in work colonies, shot whether or not they tried to resist. Secret police recruited informers with a very heavy hand; their responses to those they suspected of opposition to the regime could be exceedingly vicious. By the mid-1960s, however, these practices gradually changed. It was not that brutality was off limits—as was clear, for instance, from the fate of Gheorghe Ursu, an engineer whom the Securitate beat to death in 1985 when they found his private journal containing critical thoughts. But what was striking about Ursu's death was the rarity of such a thing by then. After 1960 brutality ceased to be the norm and subtler methods became more common, even if tougher ones reappeared as the regime tottered to its end.[8] The change meant that the consequences of the Securitate's knowledge practices became somewhat less lethal after the 1960s. Whereas previously they could have resulted in prison or exile in the gulag, now the result would be the denial of a particular job or of a passport for travel abroad.

Second, those skeptics who consider that the main products of the secret police were lies and fabrications will reject my premise that we can speak of its "knowledge practices." I beg to disagree, based on the anthropological precept that we should always take seriously the cultural categories of our research population. *Securişti* often used terms like "knowledge," "hypotheses," "information," and so on. Consider ex-officer Constantin Bucur: "This repressive apparatus, which is a good thing all over the world, departs from the idea that information is primordial. If you don't have information, you're nothing. Without information everyone turns their back on you."[9] Moreover, they did so in the context of a social system that gave knowledge special privilege. Starting with the precepts of dialectical materialism, "science" was a central concept of these regimes—if only as ideology, but that does not make it less important. Communism intended to realize the scientific management of the whole of social life; its secret police was one among many institutions enrolled in that project. As we learn from a document entitled "The Scientific Character of the Securitate's Activity Carried Out for

161

the Knowledge, Prevention, and Counteracting of All Hostile Actions," for example, "The scientific conception that governs the activity of the Securitate determines that the whole process of obtaining, verifying, and making use of information unfolds by judicious correlation and efficient use of all means and methods,"[10] and "Analysis and synthesis—scientific methods of knowledge—are used permanently at all levels of informative-operative activity."[11]

One might object that these quotations show nothing more than a language of justification, not of actual practice. No doubt science and knowledge provided a language of justification, but the evidence of the files I have read suggests that they provided a model of practice as well. *Securiști* create hypotheses, develop action plans for testing them, gather evidence, present interpretations as a result of that process, and take decisions based on those interpretations. True, their efforts begin with the presumption of a target's guilt rather than innocence, but within that framework evidence is amassed to understand better the threat he or she poses. Assuming someone is an enemy does not free one of the requirement of finding out what kind of enemy she is. In my own case, it was "evident" that I was a spy, but knowledge had to be produced indicating the nature of my activity. True, also, that often the performative dimension overtook the scientific one, as the imperatives of meeting the Plan pushed officers to demonstrate how hard they were working and the revelation of "facts" toward politically predetermined ends outweighed the analysis and interpretation of data.[12] Nonetheless, a basic goal of Securitate action was preventive—to prevent threats to social order from materializing—which required knowledge that would enable them to manipulate or influence situations and persons toward that end.[13] Officers had numerous goals beyond following individual targets, goals such as taking the temperature of the population with regular "mood reports"—their version of opinion polls. They demonstrated a veritable thirst for information, and they had many ways of obtaining it.

In proposing to describe the Securitate's knowledge practices, I do not mean to imply that these practices were acceptable: many of them were not. I mean only to take seriously their mandate to gather knowledge, so as to understand better the regime in whose service they did so. I would add, in a more personal vein, that working on this topic has not been easy, for my anthropologist's desire to treat my research population in its own terms clashes with my knowledge of the damage they wrought upon so many souls, including mine and those of my friends. Because with this project it has been more than usually difficult to cultivate distance, I unapologetically use myself to illustrate some of my points, in a kind of "auto-ethnography."

Techniques

When Major Iosif Pall offered his two hypotheses concerning me, he presented a long list of procedures that would provide proof. They relied on two senses in particular—hearing and sight—which underpinned a number of predictable measures familiar to us all, such as: intercept her internal correspondence; when she leaves her residence, shadow her; equip her rooms with special listening equipment; and so on.[14] A 1987 memo from Cluj fills this out: install listening devices at her principal contacts whom she visits at work or in their homes, as well as in her room at the "Continental" hotel, along with a video-camera to follow her activity continuously; use mobile listening devices to overhear her meetings with her close contacts in various public locales; follow her; exploit in timely fashion "microphones already in place at 'GIGI' and 'CSABA' [two Hungarian friends] so as to know continuously the discussions she will have with the respective elements; conduct secret searches to monitor her continuously and to photocopy the contents of the reports she writes."[15] It is my impression that over time, the balance shifted from technologies emphasizing sight to those emphasizing hearing. This shift accompanied a worldwide increment in surveillance technology beginning around 1970, which included miniaturized recording equipment and devices that could listen to a conversation through walls or at great distances "that in the past were in the domain of the fantastic."[16] An article in the first (1968) issue of what became *Securitatea* magazine describes some of the emerging technology, including tiny capsules placed in a telephone that enabled listening to the conversation in the room even when the telephone was hung up.[17] These items were expensive, however, and Romania could not afford as many of them as it needed—a reason why surveillance files often contain a request for permission to install such devices, which could not be left permanently in place since other officers would need them elsewhere.

Each of these techniques had its special expertise, covered in officers' coursework at the Police Academy and in instructional brochures issued by the Department of State Security. Instructions concerning the techniques for following a target are particularly interesting, as they describe the kind and color of the clothing one should wear, how to take photos through one's pocket without missing the target, use

165

of disguises, the need for superlative visual memory, how to follow someone using one, two, or three officers so the target would not detect them, and so on.[18] None of these techniques was specific to Romania; all intelligence services use them. The instructions could be quite detailed, such as indicating that when following a target into a store, the officer, "like a buyer, should look at and pick up goods" rather than standing around in a corner and looking at the people.[19] But as we learn from the Hungarian documentary "Life of an Agent," made from secret training films, officers doing this kind of surveillance could become bored and want to leave early. Moreover, the various county branches were not always up to the task of using the technology: the office in Salaj, for instance, sent to Bucharest headquarters seven recorded cassettes, which they lacked the expertise to transcribe because the people on it were talking too fast.[20]

The availability of new technology did not, however, diminish the significance of the Securitate's number one means of producing and verifying knowledge: informers.[21] A 1957 directive referring to work with collaborators states, "The basic and decisive weapon of the organs of state security, in their war against the disruptive activity carried out by the imperialist information services and internal reactionaries, is the well organized informers' network."[22] A similar document from 1976 affirms, "[The informative network] holds pride of place among the means of Securitate activity because it works consciously and is easily maneuverable, its components being recruited for their aptitudes necessary to the aims pursued by the Securitate organs and their ability to penetrate into the entourage and intimate life of hostile elements..."[23] The size, quality, and effective deployment of the informer network would determine the results of efforts to prevent, discover, and liquidate the criminal activity of enemies.[24] Also described as the "infantry on an invisible front" and the "spinal column on which are grafted and supported all the actions and measures of the Securitate,"[25] the informer network remained at the top of the list of tools throughout the communist period.[26]

Most information initially came from forcing it out of prisoners, once the Securitate became the custodian of jails in 1949. Then, following an idea drawn from the practices of NKVD head Yezhov in the 1930s Soviet Union, the Securitate began to give prisoners of certain categories—such as those with leftist sympathies— free hand to get information from their fellow prisoners. The result, known as "the Pitești phenomenon" after the most infamous Romanian prison, was devastating abuses that the prisoners wrought upon one another—and a constant flow of information for the police. In 1964, however, Romania's Party leadership declared a political amnesty, and as the prisons emptied out, the Securitate had to find new sources. Increased recruitment of informers was the result. The need was significant, for with the period of superpower détente that began in the late 1960s, the number of visitors to Romania from western countries rose exponentially (from 590 citizens of capitalist countries in 1956 to 260,000 in 1967, according to one report[27]) and with it the concern that some of them were there to spy and to corrupt Romanians. But foreigners were not the only objects of informers' attentions: they were also needed for their fellow citizens. Officers went from having fifteen-to-twenty informers each in the period between 1948 and 1968 to having as many as fifty.[28]

One thing driving the increase was pressure from above for "socialist competition" in the production plan, motivating officers to recruit more informers and open more case files. Securitate historian Cristian Troncotă writes that each year's recruitment plans had to exceed the previous year's, producing quantity at the expense of quality, and "Thus, the cruel reality of socialist competition was fully manifest in the domain of 'Secu work.'"[29] An additional impetus for enrolling more informers came from the 1974 policy of the "war of the entire people,"[30] mentioned in my Introduction, which made the whole populace responsible for ferreting out secrets and aimed to expand the informer network to encompass the whole society. Had it worked out, this policy would have considerably cheapened the job of surveillance, since informers were paid little or nothing in comparison with the officer corps.

The trajectory over time, then, was for an increase in the numbers of informers, starting in the mid-1960s. During the 1980s, however, it became ever more difficult to recruit them,[31] a fact Troncotă attributes to widespread alienation from both the increasingly repressive Ceaușescu dictatorship and the Securitate that upheld it.[32] Probably in consequence, efforts were redoubled to recruit informers in the countryside,[33] where they had always been underrepresented, and among schoolchildren.

Informers and Their Officers

What do we know about the relation of officers to their informers? Relatively little, for those two categories of people seldom write memoirs.[34] Other sources consist of instruction manuals for officers, the files of informers (accessible to researchers, in Romania), and the occasional conversation, including a few with informers in the CNSAS Oral History Archive. Using these sources, Romanian researchers such as Mihai Albu, Cristina Anisescu, and Florian Banu have provided a picture of officer-informer relations that includes the following. I refer primarily to the informers recruited among the general population, not to the special categories of collaborators who did not have to sign a pledge (*angajament*)—people such as Party members (according to regulations, they could be recruited as regular informers only with the permission of the Party) or other so-called "trustworthy people" (*persoane de încredere*).[35]

Sometimes an officer and informer knew each other from earlier occasions (school, recreational contacts), but where they did not, the process of contact and recruitment might be either brief or protracted, perhaps even involving excursions and other time spent together.[36] As I indicated in chapter 2, officers first gathered extensive information about a prospect and decided ahead of time what modality would be most effective with him or her: appeals to patriotism, veiled threats, use of compromising information or material (such as the person's having had unreported contact with a foreigner), and so on. Under-cover officers might spend several months creating friendly relations with a person they intended to recruit. Ex-officer Ţârlescu remarks that he would take a candidate to a bar or restaurant and pay for their consumption, "so as to gain ascendancy over him. You begin psychologically, get the upper hand, make him feel obligated to you."[37]

Although our prevailing image—and with good reason—of the relations between informers and officers is that they were dark, repressive, and suffocating, there is some evidence that these relations might also be somewhat friendly, involving loans of money as well as occasional gifts, including cognac, wine, ceramic vases, books, and even works of art (all provided by the organization).[38] Glaeser tells us from his interviews with Stasi officers that their meetings might include not only socializing but "rituals of virility: smoking a pack of Orient, then the GDR's most expensive cigarette brand, while drinking a good half bottle of cognac."[39] In general, the relationship was exclusive—an informer worked with only one handler, because of conspirativity—but if an agent were promoted or transferred he would turn his stable of informers over to someone else. Informers were not always willing, however: from Ţârlescu we learn that sometimes when an officer's assignment changed and he called in his informer to pass him along to a new handler, the informer would reply, "'No, sir, I was friends with you and I don't want to [work with someone else].' There were cases like that."[40]

171

Securitate training manuals envision the relation as pedagogical: the officer trains his informers, molds and develops them, shapes their personal qualities. An instruction for officers urges that they not regard their informers as "petty-bourgeois bandits" but rather "as people with their own problems, their own aspirations, their various ways of seeing the world, whom we, as Securitate organs, not only must use for our own ends to uncover the enemy but, at the same time, must educate as well."[41] He responds to their problems beyond just those related to informing and is to keep in mind their vulnerabilities and emotions. Instructions prescribe what attitude the officer should have: to be comradely but not too familiar, and to create relations of cooperation that enable the informer to feel he is contributing to something important. The officer teaches his informers new skills, such as new concepts, a new language, how to read between the lines and anticipate responses, how to become an agent of manipulation.[42] Ex-informer Nicolae Corbeanu writes that his officer even taught him how to avoid giving compromising information: after numerous meetings in which he had little to report, the officer told him that he should simply write in his informative note, "Nothing to relate (*nimic de semnalat*)." He also advised Corbeanu that if he did not want to give information on his contemporaries, he should report on his relatives in France, using information from their letters, which were undoubtedly read by the Securitate even before he got them.[43] Such advice serves to complicate our picture of officer-informer relations.

The informer should have no personal secrets and should discuss his mistakes, sins, and opinions with the officer, who exploited the information and offered him guidance. Often the informers were themselves shadowed or verified, using other informers or tape recording their conversations at home, to see whether they were truthful[44] in their reports and attitudes. As Albu puts it, "The fact that you were a Securitate collaborator did not place you above suspicion."[45] The relation of officer to informer was not a partnership, a relation of mutual trust,[46] even though the officers often presented themselves as "friends," and informers were instructed to sign messages for them as "friend" or "colleague."[47] In cases in which the informer was recruited through compromising material (homosexual activity, an illegal abortion), the relation might appear to be a kind of exchange—the officer would suppress the compromising material in exchange for the informer's supplying information—but the exchange was not equal, and the informer too was expected to suppress information: about his collaboration with the officer.

173

If this is the tone of the instructions and informer files, what evidence is there about actual relations of officer to informer? One of the people who informed on me, "BENIAMIN,"[48] described his recruitment as having been conducted in a very welcoming manner. The officer emphasized how valuable his talents and qualities were and how his country needed people like him to help, offering to help him in exchange. His handler did indeed give him friendly assistance and advice, especially concerning his career choices (guiding him in a certain direction useful to the organization, however). As their relationship continued, the officer frequently praised him, working with him on his reports and making him feel important, expressing interest in his personal life. But then sometimes he would berate and chastise "Beniamin" for not having given him some information he needed, and he was often very insistent with his assignments, as if "Beniamin," a very busy person, had no other claims on his time. Nonetheless, "aside from some very subtle moments that indicated I HAD to do what he said, otherwise he acted as if we were friends."

Especially interesting was "Beniamin's" answer to my asking whether he became close to his handler. He hesitated, then said, "No, but I had the impression that he knew absolutely everything about me. He seemed to be of above average intelligence, particularly in his ability to synthesize my ideas. He would ask me questions, then say, 'Let's write this out,' and summarize what I had said, rephrasing my scattered thoughts in concise and detailed language, which I would then write down." This practice required the informer to appropriate the officer's language and angle of vision as his own actively, thereby shaping his thought. "Beniamin" was indeed aware sometimes that he was being manipulated in a specific direction: "'Katherine Verdery is an enemy, it's certain she's hiding something,' and he did in fact plant doubts in me about you."

In "Beniamin's" recounting of it now, even though he admired the officer's intelligence and powers of synthesis, their association also filled him with terrible anxiety and produced stomach aches and sleepless nights whenever he had a meeting scheduled the next day. My friend Mariana reported exactly the same thing: the torment of waiting for the inevitable phone call from the officer whenever I came to visit, and then of waiting for the meeting they had set up, usually following a sleepless night. Because he required that she meet him in a restaurant distant from both her residence and her work, using transportation lines that did not readily intersect, each such visit required a significant investment of time, prolonging the experience of anxiety.

175

What qualities made someone a likely candidate for recruitment as an informer? Extremely important were their sociability and social connections. From my file it is evident that as soon as officers learned I was growing close to someone, they targeted that person for recruitment as an informer. Moreover, as a general principle, many people not just in Romania but in all of Eastern Europe became informers because they had friends and families whom they wanted to protect. That is, they became informers *because they were deeply embedded in social ties.* The Securitate selected them for recruitment for the same reason: documents from the archives instruct that the best people to recruit as informers are those who are well connected.[49] Here is a comment from the recruitment file of a schoolboy, concerning the investigation into his suitability: "It emerged that he is sociable and has many acquaintances among the other pupils, enabling him to bring to our attention aspects outside of school as well."[50] Former officer Victor Mitran notes a preference for older people as informers because they had more free time, could stand in queues and overhear people, were disposed to circulate a lot, and entered easily into gossip with others.[51]

According to Anisescu, officers aimed to control the informer's social world, "which implied controlling information and modalities of relating as well as an exact knowledge of the informer's physical, familial, professional, and social environment."[52] A crucial means of control was the oath that informers were required to sign, stating that they would never reveal the secret of their collaboration to anyone, including friends and family. [53] Keeping this oath meant having to lie to intimates about where one was going and what one was doing. The officer was to instruct every informer closely on plausible justifications for the time when they were meeting with him, such as having to resolve something at work, going to a sports event, buying something, and so on. (One wife, unpersuaded by her husband's explanations and convinced that he was having an affair, followed him to his meeting with his handler—which ended his informing.[54]) Thus, becoming an informer affected a person's other relationships, not only by interposing the officer between the informer and the people he was now following (who might be relatives or close friends), but through this oath of secrecy that separated him from *all* his normal contacts.

I observed earlier that surveillance techniques relied on two senses, hearing and sight. Creating informers involved manipulating both. First was their visibility: if informers were "infantry on an invisible front," it was not the informers themselves who were

177

invisible but their relationship to the organization. The latter had to remain invisible, setting up the informers as its visible edge while hiding their connection. Second, that invisibility was purchased with silence, and it had obvious repercussions on the informer's social world. My friend Mariana described to me how her recruitment to inform on me had affected relations with her friends. The *Securişti* had concluded their meeting by ordering her to sign an oath that she would never say anything about it to anyone. A very sociable woman with many friends, Mariana found it terrible to have to hide from them both what had happened to her that night and the ongoing saga of having to report on me. Then she said,

> Two or three days after the [1989] revolution, my first subject of conversation with my friends Adriana and Ionel was what had happened to me the night I was recruited. I had never told anyone, and it was deeply liberating to tell them now. We had always talked about "us" and "them," and once I had made this confession I thought we could all remain "us"—I kept insisting that I was never *involved* in the reporting, I hadn't become "them." I had to make my confession or our friendship couldn't continue. I needed their understanding, their absolution. Like with a priest.[55]

These examples indicate how the injunction to silence displaced informers' allegiances away from their own network and toward their relation with their handler. In addition, meetings with the officer cut into an informer's time for friends and non-work activities. If Mariana had agreed, as her handler wished, to report on other people besides me, the detriment to her social relations would have been even greater. Finally, her relation with her officer introduced a deceitful relation to herself, one she has trouble acknowledging even now, telling me, "I simply cannot think of myself as an informer." In a sense, being an informer obscured her from herself. When I asked "Beniamin" whether he had ever told anyone about his informing, he said firmly, "No." The officer had made it crystal clear that if he did, very bad things would happen to him. And besides, he added, "Why would I tell anyone? I was doing something horrible, and I knew it. This was not something I could be proud of, so why let anyone know?"

Informers' Agency

Did people approached as informers have any room for maneuver? We should break this question down into at least two parts: could people refuse to inform, and if they agreed to inform did they have any latitude in their work. Nicolae Corbeanu, quoted in chapter 2 on the question of why he did not refuse, mentioned (in addition to the terror the Securitate inspired) the element of surprise: he had no time to compose himself between realizing what the meeting was about and being told to sign. Also, he had no idea what might happen to people who refused: "If someone had told me of even a single case of someone who refused to become a snitch without ending up in jail or worse, I think my attitude would have been different."[56] The idea was well entrenched in his head that you cannot oppose the Securitate. But as Mihai Albu makes clear in his study of informer files, despite their fear and being caught off guard some people *did* refuse to become informers. He points out, first, that officers' recruitment plans always included a strategy to withdraw without blowing their cover if the meeting were not going well. Therefore, he concludes, "Securitate officers had in mind, every time, that they could be refused!"[57] In only one of the several plans he presents were any consequences mentioned for the refuser, and he finds no evidence that refusers suffered anything more than pressure or harassment (though the files may not be the best source for learning about this).[58]

Second, Albu provides examples of refusals that officers themselves supplied in their reports of recruitment attempts, such as from a person who agreed to inform but refused to sign any oath since as a man of honor and integrity, he considered his word sufficient; from another who justified his refusal on the basis that his conscience did not permit it and he was very busy with his job and family; and from a third who actually wrote out and signed his refusal: "[I] the undersigned H.H. refuse to give information to the Securitate, inasmuch as it is not in my character."[59] We could add to this other, more celebrated refusals, such as that of Nobel-Prize winning writer Herta Müller—whose rebuff of the invitation to inform, contrary to Albu's picture of things, seems to have cost her her job[60]—as well as the strategy used by famed pastor László Tőkés (an instigator of the 1989 revolution) when pressured into becoming an informer: he signed an agreement and then, contravening its stipulations, told all his associates that he had been interrogated and recruited.[61] An elaborate system for refusing to collaborate emerges from Tabajdi and Ungváry's comparison of the relation of the Catholic Churches of East Germany and Hungary to the state security. Whereas two-thirds or more of the Hungarian bishops and archbishops agreed to collaborate, all but one of the East German Church leaders refused. How did they manage it? In each East German diocese the bishop chose one priest to communicate with the Stasi, prohibiting everyone else from direct communication and obligating the priests to inform their leaders immediately if they were approached or recruited by the secret police. Moreover, the Church hierarchy proclaimed that there must be *at least two* Church people in any meeting between the Church and any representative of a state organ.[62]

It is important that, in contrast to my comments about initiation in chapter 2 emphasizing the transmission of secret knowledge downward (from higher- to lower-level initiates), the entire knowledge production effort of the Securitate rested on the opposite movement: of "secret" knowledge upward from informer to officer and on up the chain of command. Whereas the presumption had been that the senior partner to an initiation had knowledge the junior did not, now that was reversed: the junior partner, especially the lowly informer, held the secret knowledge desired by the senior partner. In the first model, powerful elders exert their power by withholding information from juniors. Anecdotal evidence suggests that informers too saw themselves as having some power based in withholding—that is, they had some space for initiative, for they had information the officer needed, and they could hold it back. In informer files Albu finds examples suggesting forms of "tacit resistance," as people wrote inoffensive notes they thought would do no harm, thus seeking to wash away some of the stigma of collaborating.[63] Vatulescu quotes a Securitate report that complained about informers "who provide materials of small importance, skirt the fulfilment of their tasks, do not attend meetings regularly, etc."[64] For East Germany, Garton Ash reports that one of his informers said "he really thought these were innocent little fragments."[65] Another one told him that she chatted away with her officer, "giving all sorts of harmless detail."[66] My informer Mariana said that her goal became trying to outwit them, giving them information of little use and being silent about more important things.

Despite their training, however, it was not always possible for an informer to know what an officer would find important. As Garton Ash replied to his informer, "It was precisely those tiny fragments they were interested in. Afterward they put them together, like archaeologists constructing a Roman pot."[67] Anisescu writes, "The anodyne could become the signifier of danger or betrayal," and "often the banal fact was deliberately transformed into something extremely dangerous."[68] My friend Mariana, in whose house I inadvertently left my most closely guarded field notebook, leapt at the chance to tell her handler that she had looked at it and found nothing important; she thought she was protecting me. But the result of her disclosure was that the officers now *knew* about the notebook (which was almost always on my body) and managed to get it and copy it, I still don't know how. It was true, then, that structurally the informers had some power, but not understanding the officers' knowledge practices kept them from being able to make effective use of it.

Over time, the informer could withdraw from collaborating by gradually agreeing to fewer and fewer meetings, or make himself difficult to contact, or simply not show up for meetings that were scheduled.[69] Examples of indolent informers proliferate. An officer's note from 1957 comments on an informer who had "not exerted the slightest effort or respected the tasks assigned him, since in several informative notes he signals exactly the same thing, which leaves the impression that he prepared fictitious notes not based on real facts."[70] For Hungary, Tabajdi and Ungváry write that in an important case, strikingly many informers "avoided the actual work. Out of the seventy [informers] who were assigned on this case, only seven individuals gave more than eight reports."[71] Then we find informers who withdrew outright, leaving in their informer file a signed note saying, "I refuse to collaborate any more" or an officer's report indicating something like, "He let us know that he is no longer in a position to help us with informative work."[72] An extreme case was one man who wrote, following a pathetic account of the sad circumstances that had led him to sign up in the first place:

> For three years you have been receiving from me jottings in accord with the truth, uncorrupted by any subjectivism, concerning people I mostly consider to be in some cases windbags, in others disgusting. [...] I cannot stand myself any more, I'm on the verge of a nervous breakdown and suffer devastating insomnia, I'm killing myself. Think of me as you will, correctly or no, treat me fairly or brutally, take measures to liquidate me or view me as a basket case, show me kindness or supreme harshness, spare me or not, but from this day forward I can no longer assist you in this way, I can no longer continue this job that provokes in me such immense self-loathing.[73]

Networks and Patrons

Officers used informers to gain knowledge of the behavior, attitudes, and dispositions of particular targets, knowledge that the officers then developed into a picture of those targets. As I noted in chapter 1, this picture was not aimed simply at finding evidence of a specific crime but at showing a *propensity* for criminal

185

activity. Their goal was to create a comprehensive bi-ography of the person being followed, based on re-cording as much of the target's activity as possible. In reports from someone close to me: "On 24-Nov-1974 the [American] was invited to dinner at [X], where she stayed all evening." "On 19-Nov-1974, af-ter she returned from town she went to [Y]… say-ing that she needed to calm her nerves." "On 27-Nov-1974, the American citizen went to the post office to mail a package…" In a report from a good friend: "I saw her by chance in town in the car of the Roman Catholic Hungarian bishop of Arad. She says Buda-pest is a beautiful city, where she stayed for two days before coming here." And from someone else: "The whole time she was here there were reservations about her because she's of Hungarian origin."[74] Indeed, no detail was inconsequential….

The informer's role could go beyond simply col-lecting data, however, to actually shaping the tar-get's attitudes and behavior. A prime means for this was exerting "positive influence." In my own case, for example, the instructions given to academic in-formers repeatedly emphasize that they are to influ-ence my work in a positive direction, away from the negative and hostile interpretations they fear I am generating. "Informer 'Păun' was given the task of getting close to her, to continue the process of positive influence and to guide and orient her, so she conceives her work in the spirit of historical truth and presents it objectively, not tendentiously or with mystifications."[75] An informer's note indicates that "Thanks to professor [X], she's reoriented her work in a more productive direction."[76] With examples like this we move from simple information gathering to the transformative effects of Securitate knowledge practices: how they manipulated their informers into becoming agents of social change who modified the social environments of their targets, with potential consequences for those targets' very selves. (I realize that my language may render informers more passive than they were, but I am concerned for now with the practices of officers.)

To see this, it is helpful to indicate how the Securitate, as members of the larger Romanian society, conceptualized the nature of their object of study: human beings, or persons. In Romania as in other socialist societies, persons were not conceived of as "autonomous individuals," in a western mold. Instead, as Elizabeth Dunn has argued for Poland, they were understood as *socially embedded*: as composites of all the social relations running through them—as "dividuals," in Marilyn Strathern's language, or partible persons.[77] That is, personhood was divisible, not unitary. Accompanying this difference was a difference in two kinds of disciplinary force: one, associated with the personhood of "autonomous individuals," is based on interior, often unconscious states (like guilt) within the individual subject, and another, associated with partible or embedded personhood, rests on an external network of observers who discipline by their "diminishing or disapproving gaze."[78] Autonomous individuals discipline themselves, embedded persons are disciplined by others.

Embedded personhood went hand in hand with a highly personalistic organization of society. As numerous commentators have observed, personalistic ties were the currency of social life in socialism.[79] Francis Spufford's novel *Red Plenty* describes the basic rule of life in the Soviet Union as "Everything is personal": "Because friends look after friends; and when you're with me, you aren't just friends with the people you do business with direct, you're friends with everyone I'm friends with. And that's enough people, I promise you, to solve virtually any problem you may have."[80] To this description we should add that a person's status and power increase as he accumulates more "friends" or clients upon whom he can depend for the favors he must hand out in turn. That is, these were not only personalistic systems but systems organized around clientelism (which, as I argued in chapter 2, intersected with secrecy in interesting ways). Although that was characteristic of socialism in general, it was especially true of Romania.

These aspects of social organization have three consequences. The first is that if persons are the sum of their relationships, then changing the configuration of their relationships changes them as well. I will return to this point in a moment. The second is that because the conceptual basis of such personalistic systems is not the individual but the network of social relationships, it was networks, not individuals, that the Securitate pursued –both for recruiting informers and for surveillance over targets.[81] Their view that the network is the proper object of intervention had a venerable lineage: Hannah Arendt reports that the Okhrana, the secret police of czarist Russia (another highly personalistic society), had filing cards with a person's name circled in red linked to other names in differently colored circles for the different kinds of friends and acquaintances, and with lines indicating cross-relations. "[T]his is the utopian goal of the totalitarian secret police," she writes in *The Origins of Totalitarianism*: instead of trying to figure out who is who or who thinks what, they aim to discover who is related to whom and with what degree of intimacy.[82] Poenaru offers an alternative phrasing: "In the Soviet system, the individual is never guilty as such, as an isolated human

189

being, but always [as] part of a 'guilty' wider set of social relations."[83]

Since networks were intrinsic to socialism, then the Securitate could readily mine them for the relationships essential to it. Their word for these relations was *anturaj*, "entourage." Recruiting a new informer would entail close study of his entourage, including his relatives out to the fourth degree. Pursuit of a target required discovering her entourage, which would help to reveal what kind of enemy activity she was engaged in and would produce new targets for investigation. In this respect a key Securitate research method was what sociologists call "snowball sampling," in which a person being followed would lead them to people she met or corresponded with, as Vultur found in reading her own Securitate file.[84] (See Figures 3.1 and 3.2.)

The third consequence of Romania's personalistic social organization was that *Securişti* had a model—patronage—for their relations with informers. Like everyone else, officers were enmeshed in patronage relations. The most spectacular such case involved the deputy head of Foreign Intelligence, General Ion Mihai Pacepa, who prior to his defection in 1978 supposedly courted many well-placed Party officials with gifts and thereby eluded the control to which his unit should have been subject.[85] But personalism existed at all levels below that: Officer Ţârlescu, for example,

Figure 3.1. Photograph of some people in "VERA's" entourage

191

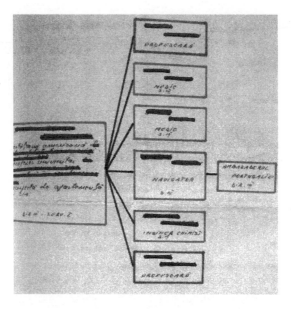

Figure 3.2. Officer's diagram of a US researcher's entourage (names and source withheld at the researcher's request). Contacts in red are already under surveillance by a branch of the Securitate, indicated near the bottom of each box.

complained in his interview about agents who are suddenly promoted, "somebody's friend, so they get advantages, a big salary…"[86] An officer's stable of informers might take on something of a clientelistic quality, too. According to former officer Victor Mitran, "The most substantial recompense [for informing] was not monetary; it consisted of the help that Securitate cadres offered these informers in resolving certain personal or family problems, problems irresolvable through official channels."[87] Officers seduced people into informing by promising them assistance, and as reported by officer Constantin Hulubaş, an important reason some people agreed to collaborate was to ensure "that they would 'have someone,' who could help if needed."[88] (I will have more to say later about the constraints on this possibility.) In Romania, "having someone" was the most valuable resource imaginable.

If targets were enmeshed in relations forming their entourage, the word used to describe relations between officers and their stable of informers was, rather, *reţea*, or network. This network had some peculiar properties. For instance, unlike the entourage of an informer or target, many of whose associates knew one another (their network had high integration, in the language of network analysis), the informers who were linked to an officer never knew anyone but him: that was a requirement of conspirativity. Other characteristics of these networks, such as their degree of hierarchy or centralization and the frequency and density of connection, would be significantly affected by the increased number of informers that was planned as of the 1970s. Unless the size of the officer corps were also increased, each officer would now have more informers than he could easily see with any frequency. For example, when Victor Mitran moved to the Investigation bureau in Bucharest in 1973, he claims to have inherited sixty informers and some five hundred collaborators![89] If meetings with an informer usually lasted up to two hours,[90] we can readily see that increasing the informer load would push the officer in the direction of less frequent and shorter encounters, to which the informer would have to come with his notes already written, rather than writing them under the officer's guidance at their meeting. That, however, posed problems of conspirativity, for an informer's notes might be seen by someone in his home or workplace where he was writing them. Increased numbers would also attenuate the officer's educational role and his ability to behave like a patron, solving problems as promised for his too-numerous informers. One solution was to interpose another level in the management of informers: the use of so-called residents (*rezidenți*), experienced and trusted informers who were given the task of meeting with some of an officer's network and reporting the results to him. This too compromised conspirativity by increasing the number of people who knew an informer's identity. In addition, it increased both hierarchy and decentralization.

In a clientelistic environment, officers' relations with informers also had some peculiar characteristics, for the officer's training placed important constraints on his ability to act like a patron. We see a hint of these constraints in a 1951 instruction for creating informers in the villages. To build personal relations, the officer must stop people on the street and chat with them; he is to become friendly with peasants by paying to sleep at their house, to eat their food, to rent a cart and horse—and he should do these with many different peasants, so as to create many relationships. This will help to disguise the identities of those informers he is able to recruit, since he will be seen with many different people. But unlike the usual patron, he is not to create familiarity or to make any promises about help he might be able to offer, but tell his informers with problems that their resolution is not within his competence; anything he does promise has to be cleared with a superior. During his meetings with the informer, the officer must be reserved, and in the interests of conspirativity he is forbidden to have any relations with the informer other than those of work.[91] In brief, *he is supposed to create personalistic relations with villagers but not behave in accordance with personalistic norms.*

We see the contradictions nicely in Glaeser's discussion of the informers the Stasi recruited to monitor and disrupt East Germany's dissident movement:

On the one hand the informants had frequent, long, and intensive contact with a set of people who were supposed to be anti-authorities... they ate with them, drank with them, laughed with them, played

195

with their children, listened to music together... On the other hand, they met one single officer, often several times a week, who for the most part was not a friend, a buddy, but in crucial ways knew more about them than anybody else. That officer had to remain a bureaucrat, even if he also once in a while cooked for them, received them with coffee and sweets at their meetings, but who had, after all, a job to do, a report to write that had to follow a particular script to satisfy his superiors. The informants were thus sandwiched between people who thought and acted like friends even though they were supposedly enemies, and an officer who was a comrade, who, qua rules and regulations, was not supposed to become a friend or even an intellectual partner because his eyes had to remain fixed to the particular goals of the casework.[92]

I insist on the atypicality of the relation of officers and informers, which fit the standard model neither of patronage nor of friendship, in order to move to my main argument about informers as tools of knowledge production: namely, that their use was parasitic upon basic forms of social life in Romania (as well as elsewhere in Eastern Europe) while pushing those forms in new directions related to the Party's aim of creating the "new socialist person." The Securitate was instrumental in realizing that aim, in ways I think scholars have not adequately appreciated. In order to gain knowledge, officers manipulated social relations in very specific ways, both in their recruitment of informers and in using them to change the shape and character of the target's own social relations, so as to create networks that would have certain desired effects. To pursue this idea is to ask how political power invested itself in local networks, with the intention of turning those to its own purposes. I have already indicated something of this for the relations with informers and will now concentrate on those of targets, illustrating with examples from my own file.

Transforming Targets

Crucial to the Securitate's construction of the spy "VERA" as an object of knowledge is a deep concern with her attachments. The most basic information for them concerns networks: if they know my networks, that will reveal my truth. In their instructions to informers and in their work plans, they always want to know whom I visit and what I discuss. They comment that I am good at forming connections, and this makes them worry that I will recruit people against Romania's interests.

In attending to my contacts, *Securiști* have several goals. They seek to colonize my attachments, to introduce new ones into my circle of acquaintances, and to break up my own networks. Seeing people as the sum of relationships rather than as individuals, their technique is to make me the sum not of *my* relationships but of *theirs*, diverting me from my own social trajectory and pulling me off center. This will help to contain any damage I might do. That damage was significant, because relationships and networks were not only the Securitate's currency, they were my currency as well. Social relationships are the anthropologist's basic work instrument. I made friends, who introduced me to other friends; because I too recruited "informers," well connected people were just as valuable to me as to the Securitate. Normally, ethnographers try to integrate themselves into existing systems of relations—becoming adopted into kinship roles, and so on. But *Securiști* aimed to prevent that. To them, I was dangerous not only because I collected socio-political information (their abiding concern), but also because I disrupted existing channels of relating. I set up competing claims, alternative loyalties. How do they combat this?

First, they try to recruit my contacts for themselves—either directly, or indirectly by capturing our speech through their microphones. Instructions found in the archive specify the different categories of informers, of which the most valued were so-called depth informers (*informatori de profunzime*), who were "placed in immediate proximity" and were "recruited from among the target's intimates, having the full possibility of knowing everything they do, as well as their intentions."[93] In my case, Mariana was one such person. Second, they are eager to insert intimates into my network—though they might be careful about morality, "studying the possibilities for inserting an informer who is unmarried."[94] Planting informers near me requires discernment: officers respond to a failure to draw me into one friendship by observing, "We have to interpose sources educated in her specialty."[95] As I indicated above, their goal with these "plants" might not be just to learn my thoughts but to modify them through "positive influence."

Finally, they seek to disrupt my existing connections. In January 5, 1985, the Securitate's deputy chief, General-Colonel Iulian Vlad, ordered his subordinates to make proposals to contain the threat I posed.[96] Their response included taking special steps to *destroy my entourage*, by warning my associates not to talk with me (as the basis for these warnings, agents were to tell people what was in my field notes, which they had copied). The Securitate understood that power flows in social relationships, that people's sociality is dangerous and must be disrupted, to contain potential threats. *Securiști* were to sever a target's relations to his or her world by introducing informers and false friends to neutralize their activities. (The same principle applied to people recruited as informers also: according to one informer, by the time she agreed to inform, following months of grueling exertion by two officers, she had few friends left: officers had launched the rumor that she was a Securitate collaborator, thus almost completely destroying her entourage.[97])

Cristina Vatulescu helps us to understand the stakes of the tactic of disrupting people's networks. According to her, it accompanied the 1970s spread of new surveillance technologies that I mentioned earlier, which enabled gathering much more detailed information with the use of listening devices. Attention shifted from arresting and punishing people to "manipulation, discreditation, dispersion, and warning/intimidation."[98] The first and last of these aimed to influence targets positively and get them to change their behavior, whereas discrediting them and dispersing their networks aimed to isolate them, severing their relations to the surrounding world so their activities could not affect it. "Isolation became a key word both in administrative documents and in the files themselves.... This attempt to control and enfeeble the suspect's connections is epitomized by... the detailed list

of the suspect's relationships…emphasizing the oblig-
atory inclusion of close family members. Through this
list, each file became the potential originator of other
files in an arborescent model that first takes over the
family tree and later threateningly spreads out to '*any*
inimical *and* personal relationships.' It is then the relationship that is inimical…the interpersonal that is
criminalized and targeted."[99]

Some readers might object that with these observations about monitoring networks and isolating
targets, I have merely reproduced the "social atom-
ization" thesis made famous by the old totalitarian model. I believe I am doing something more.[100]
In keeping with Holquist's observation at the head
of this chapter that the purpose of surveillance was
to change people, I have been showing that the regime was not simply disintegrating social relations but
striving to reforge them, thereby altering the kinds of
human beings they enmeshed. *Securiști* intended to
create new contacts for people while disrupting older ones: their aim was not just to obtain knowledge
but to transform the conditions under which information would be produced. They did not simply *harvest*
what came from their stable of informers concerning
targets: they sought to *induce* networks *around* their
targets. Standard analysis of networks envisions them
as lines connecting sets of dots (people) that preexist

201

the line drawn between them. But the network lines the Securitate sought to forge did not link dots already there: they *created* the dots and connected them through lines whose vector was not the target's life but the Securitate's intentions.[101]

I mentioned above that Romanian cultural conceptions understand persons as embedded in social relations, and that the notion of discipline appropriate to this conception relies less on inner individual conscience than on the disapproving gaze of others. In this context, the Securitate officer's task was to substitute for those others' approving/disapproving gaze his own and that of the Party, always on the lookout for "enemies." Hence the emphasis on separating both informers and, through them, the broader citizenry from their other social relations—on refocusing their networks according to the Party's patriarchal vision. Securitate work rested on the assumption that because knowledge flows in a network, networks must be cut, carefully removing people from their accustomed relations and attaching them to new ones. Those new relations would then recenter the person's networks on invisible Securitate agents and their informers, enabling officers to control the flow of knowledge more easily. But if, as I suggested earlier, people are seen as the sum of their relations, *this recentering will alter them as persons*. In this way the transformations the Securitate wrought were basic to the project of forming the "new socialist person" attempted by every Communist Party in the Soviet mold. This "person" would not be a social atom—certainly not in Romania—and it would be shaped in keeping with new kinds of political kinship and family that the Securitate mediated in the Party's service. We can see this more clearly by exploring the model of social relationships I believe the Securitate employed in their attempts to reshape the social field.

A Securitized Society

Social relations have many idioms, which recruit people for many different purposes and involve a variety of loyalties and obligations. They can be based in kinship, in locality, in workplace, school ties, neighborliness, political affiliation, and ethno-national or religious identification. Some are chosen voluntarily, others are not. Central to many of them is that they connect people directly, in both vertical and horizontal webs. To be your schoolmate means for me to be connected to you directly by shared experiences and to the teachers and other classmates we knew; our relationship to each other does not have to go through our teacher in order to link us (see Figure 3.3). But

203

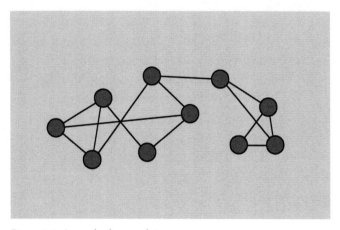

Figure 3.3. A standard network image

I believe the Securitate's idea of social relations differed from this. It favored the political dimension of relationships (rather than, say, kinship or school ties) and envisioned them as primarily vertical, centering on officers and their informers, who were further connected to others in society through informing (see Figure 3.4). This reflected the Party's desire to mediate all relations, to be the ultimate network node: all connections were to run through it, rather than directly from one person to another. Securitate techniques envisioned society not as a web, with links running among persons, but as a rake or three-dimensional star, with links running separately from people up to officers and the Party.

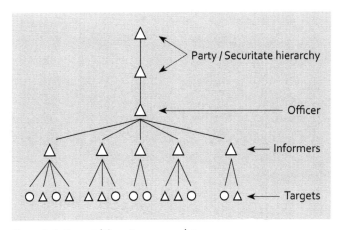

Figure 3.4. Potential Securitate network image

Above all, in place of the kinship relations so important to Romanians the Communist Party sought to create a new kind of family, a political one encompassing the whole society. Their image of family was patriarchal and hierarchically defined, with people relating to each other through the Party patriarch, personified in "Father" Nicolae Ceaușescu and his wife, Elena.[102] The Securitate's job was to implement this vision. They took the familial metaphor seriously: informer files include the recruitment of thousands of schoolchildren lured with promises in exchange for giving their loyalty to their officer, the Party, and the Ceaușescus rather than to their own families or their peers, upon whom they were to report.[103] The Securitate's "family" was itself patriarchal, the great majority of officers and most of the informers being men. But their new family was not an open and trusting one: everyone, including the officers themselves, was under surveillance.

Creating the socialist "family" entailed reducing the weight of other kinds of relations and increasing the hierarchical political relations until, ideally, they would take over social relations completely. Neagoe-Pleşa and Pleşa write,

> The [post-1965] renunciation of measures involving terror … led to the necessity of creating as vast an informative network as possible, which would permit extending surveillance over the entire society. Securitate officers in all sectors had clear instructions to create informers' networks in all their areas of responsibility. Therefore informers were recruited in every state institution, in factories, hospitals, schools, even going as far as networks by street and apartment building. All these networks permitted the generalization of informative surveillance of every person, both in the workplace and at home. As in an Orwellian scenario, all individuals had to know that the "attentive eye" of the Securitate was everywhere and none of their movements would go unobserved. The aim was to obtain a kind of self-censorship on the part of citizens, such that they

would refrain from opposing the regime for fear of being immediately discovered by the omnipresent informers.[104]

Anisescu states the same idea succinctly: "The strategy of the Securitate organs was to construct a mass cadre of informers (*agentura*); the informers' network had to be extended into the most diverse socio-professional environments, so as to have control at the level of the entire society."[105]

That ambitious hope was not unfounded. It is impossible to know exactly how many informers the Securitate disposed of, for there were many different kinds of them, both willing and recalcitrant, and many different circumstances that might lead people to write an informative note even *without* formal recruitment—including the simple act of having a conversation with a foreigner, which was a crime if not reported to the authorities.[106] This said, it appears that Romania was unusually well endowed with informers, if we take at face value the figures supplied to Romania's Parliament after 1989: 486,000 informers and auxiliary personnel (people who lent their houses for informer meetings, provided contacts, and so on), assisting the approximately 39,000 full-time employees[107]; this gives a total of about 525,000 Securitate workers for a population of 23 million, or about one Securitate worker for every 42 citizens. Compare that with the East German Stasi, who had about 93,000 full-time employees and 178,000 informers and auxiliary personnel, yielding a total of 271,000 for a population of 17 million,[108] or one Stasi worker per 62 citizens. The Securitate had fewer full-time employees but was much better served by the general populace.[109] If we eliminate from the population totals everyone under age 20 (about 30 percent of the population in 1989), assuming that most children under 20 would not be informing yet, this yields about one Securitate agent or informer per 30 adults. Given, however, that the membership of the Communist Party was about 3.5 million in the 1980s and Party members were expected to collaborate with the Securitate upon request without the creation of informer files for them, the number of citizens per Securitate worker could well be even smaller.

All secret services recruit informers, but this loose comparison between the Stasi and the Securitate indicates that in Eastern Europe there was some variation in the extent to which they did so. As someone coming from the US, that most pathologically individualistic of countries, I have always found the degree of Romanians' social embeddedness remarkable and have seen it as linked to a trait of which they are justly proud: their immense capacity for hospitality.

Was the Securitate blessed with a more fertile field than the Stasi, in having a greater wealth of sociability it could colonize among Romanians to produce its knowledge? Or does the comparison reveal, rather, a "cost-containment" strategy in Romania, of using informers (who were paid relatively little or nothing) rather than the more costly salaried employees on whom the Stasi relied more heavily?[110] Does Romania's resort to informers indicate a "putting-out system" as against the Stasi's more highly professionalized surveillance industry, which, as I noted at the beginning, generated many more kilometers of paper?[111] Answers to such questions will reward more comparative work on these offspring of the KGB.

* * *

In this chapter I have been describing a point in a historical sequence that runs from the very visible public executions witnessed by large crowds with which Foucault opened *Discipline and Punish*,[112] on to the panopticon popularized by Bentham—where vision is concentrated in a single invisible observer at the center, with the observed citizens arrayed visibly around him—and thence to socialist power, which places the *observed citizen* at the center, with multiple kinds of vigilant observers arrayed invisibly around him. The latter two forms both place citizens under surveillance, individualizing them, but differently. The differences include the intensity of the surveillance, the extent to which it enters into the individual psyche (rather than being lodged in multiple social relations external to the embedded person), and the implications for subjects' behavior as a result. Some Romanians entered into the policing of others, thickening the web of surveillance; some merely hoped their circle of friends and kin would prove loyal to them; all had to face the possibility that they might be asked to police their fellows and to decide whether doing so might protect their own networks of family and friends.

I believe the picture I have presented contributes to a critique of lustration in transitional justice, with which I opened this book. To begin with, it calls into question the position of international organizations such as the Helsinki Committee on Human Rights and the Parliamentary Assembly of the Council of Europe, which have exerted pressure on East European countries to individualize lustration—that is, to target not *categories* (all former collaborators) but *individual persons* who collaborated—based on the argument that only thus are due process and the rule of law properly served and democratic legitimacy assured. But if collaboration was quintessentially a networked phenomenon, not an individual one, as I have argued, such interventions appear misguided. The effect of individualizing accountability is to impose notions of truth-getting that do not fit the "crime." As I have sought to show here, secret police work was successful precisely to the extent that persons under socialism were *not* autonomous individuals but network nodes.

In addition, my discussion in these chapters helps to indicate why these files cannot be used unproblematically as "truth" in the service of democratization. The reasons include the organizational imperatives of socialism's secret police that pushed them to manufacture both "enemies" and collaborators and to apply a particular interpretive grid to the information they gathered. Beyond this, their systematic and often diabolical manipulation of informers not only raises questions about the value of the information those informers contributed to the archive but makes at least some of them candidates for compassion, rather than for the retribution that transitional justice has so often pursued.[113] This possibility, which might dismay some readers, emerges from seeing the Securitate's knowledge practices as a matter less of truth than of the social relationships through which they operated. My hope in disclosing these practices is to make their continuation in Romania more difficult.

211

Conclusion

The Radiant Future?

> The top-secret world the [US] government created in response to the terrorist attacks of Sept. 11, 2001, has become so large, so unwieldy and so secretive that no one knows how much money it costs, how many people it employs, how many programs exist within it or exactly how many agencies do the same work.
> —Dana Priest and William M. Arkin,
> "Hidden World"

These chapters have concerned a form of surveillance that spread from the Soviet Union into the East European states and was undermined by the collapse of that socio-political system known as "actually existing socialism." We might therefore say that this book is "about history": it deals with a type of society that no longer exists in that part of the world. While this may be so, it does not spell the end of surveillance, which is expanding at a great rate and in multiple forms in societies across the globe, including in Romania by the Securitate's successor, the Romanian Information Service (SRI).[1]

These forms have numerous sources. For citizens of the US (but true more widely), an obvious one is

213

the surveillance through which corporations seek to learn about our most intimate and detailed habits so as to manipulate us into buying their products. The "cookies" in our internet browsers that track our every move online are only one vehicle for it; "black boxes" in our automobile engines, which record numerous aspects of our driving habits, are another. A young cousin of mine had a job following customers who entered a Walmart department store; he was to take note of their every move.[2] He might spend two hours following a single customer, noting when they hesitate, when they look at something and put it back on the shelf, how many seconds or minutes they spend looking at different products and visiting different departments, and so on. My cousin would attach himself to customers when they entered and stick with them until they left. Because in the US we do not imagine that we might be followed in a department store, there seems to be no wisdom about how to shake off such a "shadow," nor are there procedures for my cousin to disguise himself to keep from being observed, as there are for the secret police officers assigned to shadow a target. My cousin's notes strongly resemble the shadowing (*filaj*) reports in my Securitate file, except that what counts as an "observable" event for him is on a much more minute scale than was true for the Securitate.

Although most Walmart customers do not realize they are being watched, users of the internet have gradually become aware that their movements are being "mined" as data for more precise commercial targeting. They know they are watched, but they cannot avoid it without renouncing use of the internet altogether; hence, one can say that they acquiesce in their surveillance semi-voluntarily. Similarly voluntary are the "smart" electronic textbooks (my favorite example) that report to the professor on whether or not students are doing the reading. "You know it's watching you," they comment uneasily.[3]

To my mind the most remarkable form of surveillance—and the most seemingly different from the Securitate's—is the explosion of social networking sites, into which millions of people world-wide have voluntarily inserted themselves since the advent of Facebook in 2004. As of June 2013, Facebook had well over one billion registered users, or one in every seven people on the planet. Many other sites had started up as well. In the US it did not take long for prospective employers to begin making use of the Facebook pages of job applicants, so as to learn more about them. In February 2012 the *New York Times* reported that 70 percent of recruitment and Human Resources professionals in the US had rejected candidates based on data found online.[4] The history department of a well-known US university denied tenure to an assistant professor who had (stupidly) written disparaging comments on his Facebook page concerning his students; similar cases have been appearing with increased frequency.[5] The *New York Times* ran a story about an Austrian citizen who asked for his Facebook file and received 1,222 pages of material he thought he had deleted from his account. He was quoted as saying, "It's like a camera hanging over your bed while you're having sex. It just doesn't feel good. We in Europe are oftentimes frightened of what might happen some day."[6] Indeed.

Although the networking sites responded to public pressure to create better protection for their users, there is plenty of room for abuse. To ensure the accuracy of its data, Facebook is now asking users to *inform on each other*, stating whether their friends have used their real names and genders when they signed up. What is noteworthy about these sites is that unlike the secret police, which built its knowledge practices on fear, the sites manage surveillance by colonizing friendship and desire. It even seems that the experience of being data-mined has itself become a source of pleasure, so eagerly do people "inform" upon themselves by giving these social media rich data on their location, their friends, their spending habits, and so on. Privacy (whose violation is one of the ways "surveillance" is defined) seems to have lost its value.

Clearly, being targeted by ads from an online business or exposing oneself to an array of "friends" is a far cry from being harassed, frightened, or beaten by the Securitate. For these new forms of surveillance, my arguments in this book are at most a cautionary tale. Perhaps we should wonder, for instance, about the more sinister uses to which some of this seemingly innocuous information could be put—on the analogy of the informers I described in chapter 3, who mistakenly thought their chatty tidbits were inconsequential. What counts, we learned there, is not the specific information collected as much as the interpretive grid, the filter used to process it, which can place seemingly innocent information in a highly unfavorable light. Like Securitate targets, people subjected to online surveillance cannot necessarily predict what that grid will be. Will they eventually experience something of the same shock as have many Romanians, who even though they believed surveillance was everywhere are appalled now that they see more concretely the full extent of it?[7]

If the forms of surveillance I have been discussing so far offer only weak analogies with Securitate practices, that is less true of a third source, stemming from the "war on terror." Its premise—common to the Securitate as well—is that terrorists or enemies can be anywhere, making potentially everyone a suspect. The result, in the United States at least, has been extraordinary increments of state capacity for keeping an eye on citizens, largely without their knowledge. Cities are full of hidden surveillance cameras. A *New York Times* story in April 2013 described the tiny webcams and other sophisticated surveillance technology now common in law enforcement.[8] The "Stealthy Insect Sensor Project" of the US military has been training bees as spies to test for chemical weapons and radiation—they pick it up on their legs and can be trained to detect specific scents, like landmines. Tiny bee-like surveillance robots can take pictures of an assembled crowd at close range, unnoticed. Joseph Masco writes that in justifying programs of this kind, the Bush administration advocated a "mosaic theory" of information threat, which assumes that "disparate items of information (particularly the innocuous and that of no obvious utility to an adversary) can nonetheless be assembled to create a whole that is more powerful than the sum of its parts. Under this theory, any piece of information is potentially a national security threat, as it is the creative linkage across bits of knowledge that is imagined to be dangerous."[9] The Securitate could not have expressed it better.

In July of 2010 the *Washington Post* published a three-part article on the top-secret intelligence community that has grown up in the US since Septem-

218

ber 11, 2001. In that year it employed 854,000 people; the National Security Administration was then processing 1.7 billion pieces of intercepted communications every 24 hours.[10] All these programs are supposed to be secret, and the expense of the operations to classify them is extraordinary.[11] Some of the *Post*'s report included items familiar from the Securitate. For instance, many security and intelligence agencies are doing the same work, "creating redundancy and waste," and the intelligence-gathering effort is riven with turf wars and intragency competition.[12] In other respects the article offers hypotheses we might suspect were true of the Securitate as well, such as that the volume of reports on the results of this domestic spying is so large that many are routinely ignored, and the handful of people empowered to oversee the entire effort cannot keep up with it.[13] The *Post* series makes one pause to wonder that plots are uncovered and acted upon at all.

In June 2013, a massive scandal broke concerning this large-scale surveillance program of the US government. Among the facts revealed were drone flights over the national territory and the collection of data from telephones and email, having the purpose not of eavesdropping on conversations, as the Securitate did, but of analyzing broad patterns of connection (in other words, networks) that include links to data on social media, in order to discern possible terrorist plots. The rationale for this kind of surveillance is comprehensible, if regrettable, and public reaction to the scandal indicated that if surveillance thwarts terrorists, many would even find it acceptable. More troubling is that numerous people interviewed on the topic said it was hard to get worked up about it, given how much surveillance they were already under at their computers.[14]

Adding together internet surveillance, social networking sites, and the search for terrorism suspects, we find a world that resonates with the one I have been characterizing in this book: a world in which people's habits and friends become tools for keeping tabs on them, manipulating them, and diminishing their freedom even while claiming to protect them. They are not the same world, but knowledge about each informs the other in sobering ways. Living in a new kind of security state requires that we specify the differences between these kinds of surveillance and the ones I have been describing, so as to render judgment on the latter and shape a politics for the former. Among those differences would seem to be the Securitate's preference for a labor-intensive "personal touch," its way of manipulating and terrorizing people into doing its work, all under the veil of enforced secrecy, whereas the US surveillance effort—of vastly greater scale—relies almost entirely on information technologies. Nonetheless, heightened secrecy practices among western democracies—and the tendency to inflate threats, so as to gain support for those practices[15]—raise the question whether the surveillance forms of socialism, far from being a historical dead end, will have helped after all to usher in the "radiant future."

Notes

Preface

1 Kligman and Verdery, *Peasants under Siege*.
2 Davis, *Fiction*, 112.
3 Horváth and Szakolczai, *Dissolution*, Chapter 8.

Introductuction

1 Thanks to Dennis Deletant for calling this poem to my attention. Note that it was published before the collapse of the Ceauşescu regime.
2 The literature on lustration is extensive. See the bibliography in Verdery, "Postsocialist Cleansing."
3 See, for instance, Nalepa, *Skeletons*; Sadurski, *Rights Before Courts*; Williams, Fowler, and Szczerbiak, "Explaining Lustration"; and the references in the next note below. For further discussion, see Verdery, "Postsocialist Cleansing."
4 In 2002, it was revealed that Prime Minister Péter Medgyessy had collaborated with the secret police. Likewise, film director Szabó was discovered in 2006 to have written informer's reports from 1957 to 1961—a fact for which he gave changing explanations. The Mécs Commission, formed by the socialists to investigate the secret police connections of government officials, was accused by the opposition FIDESZ party of being overzealous and trampling on people's dignity. Another ardent accuser was historian Krisztián Ungváry, who decided to reveal the names of police collaborators, the most eminent of whom was archbishop László Paskai of Esztergom-Budapest, an elector in the papal conclave of Pope Benedict XVI. Some of Ungváry's targets subsequently sued him, one of whom was László Kiss, a judge in the Constitutional Court whom Ungváry accused of having written secret police reports when he was a university administrator. In 2000, novelist Péter Esterházy published *Celestial Harmonies*, his tribute to his ancestors and especially his father, only to learn soon thereafter that his father had been an active police informer from 1957 to 1980; Esterházy then published *Javított Kiadás* (*Revised Edition*), seeking to ac-

223

count for his father's behavior. For information on one or more of these scandals, see Deák, "Scandal in Budapest"; Kiss, "Misuses"; Nadkarni, "Secrets," and "Generation"; Rév, "White Raincoat."

[5] Deák, "Scandal in Budapest"; Kati Marton, *Enemies*.

[6] I submitted my request in the summer of 2006; a year-and-a-half later I received confirmation that my file was ready for me, but I was unable to consult it until summer 2008. Some additional volumes were found at that time. I believe the material I have seen is fairly complete, given routine destruction of documents during the communist period (see chapter 1).

[7] See, for instance, Ardeleanu, *N. Steinhardt*; Ioanid, *Dosarul Brucan*; Tănase, *Acasă*, and *Cioran*; Tudoran, *Eu, fiul lor*; Vianu, *Exercițiu*.

[8] I will offer a more personal account of this experience than appears in the present book in *My Life as a Spy: Memoirs of a Cold War Anthropologist*, in progress.

[9] For readers who wonder what it might be like to read a secret police file, I can do no better than recommend Gilles Perrault's extraordinary novel *Dossier 51*. Although it is not organized according to the conventions I describe below, it conveys much of the feel of reading a Securitate file. It is also a superb indictment of the excesses of these organizations.

[10] See, for example, Stoler, *Archival Grain*.

[11] Archive of the National Council for the Study of the Securitate Archives (hereafter ACNSAS), Fond Documentar (FD), file 12618/vol. 1, pp. 245–245v. More of this document appears in chapter 3.

[12] David H. Price has pursued the subject of anthropology's relation to intelligence in a number of articles and books. See, for instance, his "Interlopers," and *Anthropological Intelligence*.

[13] Although English usage enables distinguishing between police "inform*ers*" and anthropological "inform*ants*" (once the standard term in my field, which most of us no longer use), Romanian has only one word (*informător*). The similarity is nonetheless arresting: both Securitate officers and I recruited informers/-ants into our work and thereby repositioned them in their social worlds. My "informers" became possible targets for the Securitate to recruit; theirs became people for me to avoid.

I might add that in another document, they note that my mini-cassette recorder is the same kind they use themselves.

14 Davis, *Martin Guerre*, vii.

15 See, for instance, Anisescu, "Dinamica," and "Comunicarea"; Glaeser, *Political Epistemics;* Gökarıksel, "Immoral Opportunist," and "Seeking Truth"; Nadkarni, "Secrets," and "Generation"; Poenaru, "Forgive Your Neighbor"; and Vatulescu, *Police Aesthetics*. Additional relevant work is still in unpublished form as dissertations in progress, such as Gökarıksel, "Of Truths, Secrets, and Loyalties," Poenaru, "Contesting," and Szűcs, "Performing the Informer."

16 For further information on this question, see Kligman and Verdery, *Peasants*, 50–58.

17 For a discussion of Soviet actions on this front even *before* the war was fully ended, see Banu, "'Strămoșii' Securității." The same picture emerges for Hungary from Tabajdi and Ungváry, *Elhallgatott múlt*, chapter 1. My thanks to Anikó Szűcs for providing me with the summary of this work, which I have referenced in this and subsequent footnotes.

18 Banu, "Secretul de stat," 52.

19 The full titles are Narodnyy Komissariat Vnutrennikh Del (NKVD) and Komitet Gosudarstvennoi Bezopasnosti (KGB). The KGB was formed under that name only in 1954, morphing from the earlier NKVD.

20 Tănase, *Elite*, 54.

21 For instance, Cosma, *Cupola*; Tăbăcaru, *Sindromul*.

22 See, for instance, Romania, Arhivele Naționale, Direcția Județeană Hunedoara, Fond Chestura de Poliție Deva, file 6/1927, 14, 19; file 72/1937, 7–8.

23 Troncotă, *Duplicitarii*, 114–15.

24 These two observations are courtesy of Virgiliu Țârău, personal communication.

25 See Carpen, "Continuitate," 24.

26 See Moldovan, "'Partiturile' represiunii," 137–39. Moldovan also argues that this easier penetration was one reason why the Securitate objected to participating in the common informational fund centered in the Soviet Union, as Poland and Bulgaria wanted.

27 Troncotă, *Istoria*, 77 ff.

[28] Troncotă, *Duplicitarii*, 14–17. The Romanian-Chinese rapprochement pushed the Soviets to initiate regular meetings with East European intelligence services, proposing a common informational system (the SOUD); Alexandru Drăghici, the head of the Securitate, refused to join it. Complaining to Gheorghiu-Dej that the KGB was trying to steal their work and uncover their agents, he stated, "We have absolutely no need for collaboration like this" (ibid., 16).

[29] Ibid., 16. In support of the idea that the Soviets were aiming at a discriminatory division of labor, he also quotes Andropov as saying that the Soviet Union would do most of the spying, schools of espionage in Eastern Europe would be dismantled, and East European intelligence services would send to Moscow any information they obtained, receiving informative syntheses in return (ibid., 16–17).

[30] Ibid., 22, 41, 126.

[31] Ibid., 37–38. Note that 1971 was also the year in which Hungary got its first computer to manage the database (Tabajdi and Ungváry, *Elhallgatott múlt*, 158).

[32] Troncotă, *Istoria*, 94. For example, in August of 1958, 45 percent of actions in the country were covered by no informers at all, and additional actions were covered inadequately. The Interior Ministry's regional office in Pitești had seven informers for 1,100 suspects being followed, Suceava had zero informers for 600 suspects.

[33] See Anisescu, "Dinamica," 41–50; Marius Oprea, *Securiştii partidului*, 29; Troncotă, *Istoria*, 91.

[34] Oprea, *Securiştii partidului*, 19.

[35] Deletant, *Ceauşescu*, 80. Similar power struggles between the secret police and Party organizations occurred in the other Eastern European countries as well, but with different timing. In Hungary, for instance, the police were subordinated to the Party from Kádár's installation in 1956 onward—a principal demand of the 1956 revolution having been the dissolution of the security service, the Államvédelmi Hatóság, or ÁVH. Although 98 percent of its employees entered the new state security organs, all of them realized that they were beholden to the Party for their jobs (Tabajdi and Ungvári, *Elhallgatott múlt*, 52–54).

[36] For one of doubtless many examples, see the discussion in Knight, *Cold War*, 170, concerning the rivalry between the NKVD and the GRU (Glavnoye Razvedyvatel'noye Upravleniye, the Main Intelligence Directorate), the overlap in their missions, and their competition for agents, information, and influence in the Kremlin. Conflicts between the CIA and FBI in the US are, of course, legendary.

[37] Some evidence of these disagreements can be found in Deletant, *Ceaușescu*; Negulescu, *Spionaj*; and Anisescu and Moldovan, *Pseudo-memoriile*. For competition among branches of the Stasi, see Glaeser, *Political Epistemics*, 501n 33.

[38] See, for instance, the acerbic commentary of military intelligence officer Victor Negulescu, *Spionaj*, 18–19.

[39] Deletant, *Ceaușescu*, 326. A side effect of Pacepa's flight was a marked increase in the quality of instruction in the Securitate officers' training school, according to former officer Constantin Bucur, who was then a student. "After Pacepa fled, they gathered everybody up who had been working on the outside; they had to find work for them [at home]." Whereas previously no one on the staff had held the rank of general, now five or six of them did. Interview with Bucur Constantin, Arhiva de Istoria Orală (AIO) CNSAS 216, interviewed by Cristina Anisescu, 15-2-2011.

[40] Troncotă, *Duplicitarii*, 34.

[41] Ibid., 43.

[42] Information in this paragraph is from Troncotă, *Duplicitarii*, 41–44. On the concept of the "entire people," see "Instrucțiuni Nr. D–00180/1987 privind activitatea de creare și folosire a rețelei informative a aparatului de Securitate," in Anisescu et al.,*"Partiturile" Securității*, 639.

[43] Interesting parallels exist with the Soviet "methodicians" who promulgated atheism, as described in Sonja Luehrmann's *Secularism Soviet Style*. Thanks to Vlad Naumescu for this suggestion.

[44] Macrakis, *Seduced*, 160.

[45] Vatulescu, *Police Aesthetics*, 46–53.

[46] For example, a former officer interviewed for the CNSAS Oral History project observed, "Especially those from the Foreign Office were

advantaged, because they came with cartons of cigarettes, with Kents and whiskey" (Ţârlescu Gheorghe, AIO CNSAS 213, Part I, 1; interviewed by Cipriana Moise, 20-02-2011).

[47] Troncotă, *Duplicitarii*, 49.
[48] See the essays collected in Jowitt, *New World Disorder*.
[49] Horváth and Szakolczai, *Dissolution*, 173–74.
[50] Ibid., 177, 181.
[51] Ibid., 176.
[52] Horváth and Szakolczai, *Dissolution*, 216.
[53] Banu, "'Strămoşii Securităţii," 484 (emphases in original).
[54] Gross, *Revolution*, 225–40.
[55] Humphrey, "Myth-making," 28.
[56] Fedor, *Russia*, 22. Thanks to Irina Nicorici for this reference.
[57] Ibid., 27.
[58] Tăbăcaru, *Sindromul*, 42.
[59] Buck-Morss, *Dreamworld*, 13.
[60] For Hungary, where the secret police were firmly under Party control by 1957, Tabajdi and Ungváry write that "the image of the enemy and the direction of its [the political police's] activity were always defined externally" (*Elhallgatott múlt*, 19).
[61] Banu, "Secretul de stat," 52.
[62] Hunt, *Politics*; Berezin, *Fascist Self*; Klumbyte, "Political Intimacy." See also R. Williams, *Sociology*, particularly his fascinating discussion of the soliloquy, pp. 139–47.
[63] Williams, *Marxism*, 128–35.
[64] Robin, *Fear*. For some other useful works on fear, see Bădescu, "Frica"; Goldstein, "Critical Anthropology"; Green, *Fear*; Nugent, "States, Secrecy"; Skidmore, "Darker than Midnight."
[65] Troncotă, *Istoria*, 18, emphasis added.
[66] Anisescu, "Comunicarea," 25. The internal quotation is from Bădescu, "Frica," 36.
[67] Glaeser, *Political Epistemics*, 2.
[68] Berezin, *Fascist Self*, 28; Foucault, *Discipline*, 3–4.
[69] Anisescu, "Comunicarea," 52 (citing Niţescu, *Sub zodia*, 351).

[70] Oprea, *Moștenitorii*, 27.
[71] See Poenaru, "Contesting," 226.

Chapter 1

[1] Herbert (Belu) Zilber, Romanian communist from the illegal period. Also known as Andrei Șerbulescu, the name under which he published the epigraph.

[2] The principal holders were the Romanian Intelligence Service (Serviciul Român de Informații—SRI), the Foreign Intelligence Service (Serviciul de Informații Externe—SIE), the Ministry of Justice, the Ministry of National Defence, and the Ministry of Administration and Internal Affairs.

[3] Source: "The European Network of Official Authorities in Charge of the Secret-Police Files: A Reader on their Legal Foundations, Structures and Activities," 2009, available on the CNSAS website at http://www.cnsas.ro/documente/European%20Network.pdf (accessed May 30, 2013). The microfilms are important because they may include some paper files that were destroyed.

[4] All present and former Romanian citizens can ask for their files, but not all Romanians have files and not all files are "found" for those who do.

[5] Initial estimates were 35 km, but according to personnel at the CNSAS in 2012, the total is 24 km. It is uncertain whether this reflects initial error or differences between what the CNSAS now has and the total Securitate archive at the time of the revolution.

[6] The figure for Poland is from the Polish Institute for National Remembrance (courtesy of Saygun Gökarıksel). It includes court files, prison records, and military intelligence files as well. The figure for the Stasi is from Glaeser (personal communication).

Glaeser questions the possibility of comparing these figures across countries. There are complicated measurement issues: should the number in question include personnel files, those of the guard regiment, the passport control, the bodyguards, the ordinary administrative files (officers' health records and pay records, etc.), as well as enormous numbers of duplicates (for instance, one informer report of a group meeting would go into all case files of members involved, the file of the informer, and for informational purposes here and there)? Should it include background checks on the official apparatus, on the sportsmen and women allowed to travel, on the trade representatives of state owned corporations?, and so forth. The figure of 111 km (on the official document center website (http://www.bstu. bund.de/DE/Archive/UeberDieArchive/Ueberlieferungslage-Erschlies-sung/uberlieferungslage_node.html, accessed May 30, 2013) seems to include every kind of document the Stasi ever produced, so it overestimates the total surveillance effort, while simultaneously underestimating it, because other kinds of surveillance efforts are not included.

[7] See Oprea, *Moștenitorii*, 126. Olaru and Herbstritt report: "When the Berlin Wall fell on November 9, 1989, Securitate officers resident in Berlin were called back home to describe what was happening, and they told of the occupation of Stasi headquarters; rumors spread that planes were landing in Bucharest with documents from the Stasi archive" (Olaru and Herbstritt, *Stasi și Securitatea*, 199–200). The gap of six weeks between the fall of the wall and the Romanian events of December 22 gave the Securitate ample time to begin preemptive destruction of their own archive.

[8] Normal administrative practice was to destroy documents periodically, after the passage of set periods of time or after handwritten notes had been typed up and approved (the originals might then be burned). For example, Chiva and Albu report that after five years, eavesdropping material in the files would normally be purged (Chiva and Albu, *Noi și Securitatea*, 46).

[9] For example, the Central University Library of the University of Bucharest suffered heavy fire damage during the December 1989 "revolution," and it was rumored that the building's attic had contained Securitate documents. The most celebrated incident was reported in early 1990, when Securitate documents partially destroyed by fire were discovered loosely buried in the village of Berevoiești.

[10] See Poenaru, "Forgive Your Neighbor," 3, for further discussion.

[11] Trouillot, *Silencing the Past*.

[12] Poenaru, "Forgive Your Neighbor," 11.

[13] Kotkin, *Magnetic Mountain*, 367; see also Lefort, *Political Forms*, 297–302.

[14] Poenaru, "Forgive Your Neighbor," 11.

[15] Şerbulescu, *Monarhia*, 144, 146.

[16] For more information on officer-informer pedagogy, see Gökarıksel, "Immoral Opportunist," 11.

[17] Alexei Yurchak describes several hoaxes in which people make a fraudulent claim by directing attention away from its intrinsic meaning and to the flawlessness of the documents supporting it. These hoaxes indicate that *how* something is presented outweighs *what* was presented, and they expose the hidden cultural principle that gives truth-value to something because it is articulated in authoritative form. See Yurchak, "Parasite," 322–23.

[18] Hull, *Government of Paper*.

[19] Vatulescu, *Police Aesthetics*, 13.

[20] See, for instance, Tănase, *Acasă*, for Romania; Marton, *Enemies*, for Hungary. Marton observes concerning her parents' file in Hungary: "Such utterly wasted human effort… . The hundreds of man-hours agents in two capitals devoted to assessing the best way to intercept my mother on her daily drive" (224). Radu Ioanid ("Anatomia delaţiunii"), writing of his own file, says that the recordings of his telephone calls "indicate a tremendous waste of technical and human means, with embarrassing results for those who ordered it."

[21] I wonder whether they *really did* wait—most Romanians of my acquaintance would have found a way to avoid doing that. Precisely this expectation on my part contributed to my not taking the Securitate's surveillance practices seriously enough.

[22] ACNSAS, Fond Informativ (FI), Dosar de Urmărire Informativă (DUI) 195851/1, 183–92 (from 1974).

[23] Garton Ash reports that the Stasi officers he spoke with commented on the very long days demanded by their work (Garton Ash, *The File*, 190), as does Glaeser (*Political Epistemics*, part 3, esp. 315–16).

[24] Corbeanu, *Amintirile*, 290.

231

[25] See, for example, Albu, *Informatorul*, 17, giving a document that mentions a recruitment plan of ten informers of which only three have been obtained; another document mentions the inflation of the recruitment plan for the subsequent year.

[26] Conspirativity underlay the necessity of recruiting both informers (since targets were not supposed to know their case officers) and other collaborators—such as from the postal service, because other postal workers were not supposed to know about means of censoring correspondence. "Directiva referitoare la cenzura secretă a corespondenței, 1954," in Anisescu et al., *"Partiturile" Securității*, 346, 347, 364.

[27] Oprea, *Moștenitorii* , 52–53.

[28] My thanks to Maya Nadkarni for providing me with this film.

[29] See "Ordinul Ministrului Afacerilor Interne al Republicii Populare Române nr. 85 și Instrucțiunile privind supravegherea operativă organelor M.A.I.," in Anisescu et al., *"Partiturile" Securității*, 411. Gail Kligman reminds me that the practice of crossing streets was mirrored in everyday life. When people thought they detected a *Securist*, they would cross the street. Kligman recalls turning it into a game, especially in the late '80s when she was tailed all the time and street crossing became part of her ritual. She would pretend to window shop (even though the stores were empty); across the street, her "tail" would stop. Then she would cross the street, and he would do the same

[30] Bălan, "Preocupări," 33.

[31] Anisescu et al., *"Partiturile" Securității*, 401–2.

[32] Olaru and Herbstritt, *Stasi și Securitatea*, 56.

[33] Troncotă, *Istoria*, 88.

[34] Bakhtin, "Discourse," xix–xx, 278–79, 428.

[35] See Troncotă, *Istoria*, 129–30, for the points in this paragraph.

[36] Not all these measures worked out as planned. For instance, a marginal note on one document from 1985 reported a lunch I had with a friend, commenting, "Because of poor quality microphones, the recording was bad so we lost lots of data that could have clarified the preoccupations of these two people." In another case, despite a massive mobilization of forces, they apparently forgot to request permission to install microphones and lost the

content of a crucial conversation. See ACNSAS, FI, DUI 195847/4, 85–86. Concerning the latter example, writer George Ardeleanu, reporting on my visit to Nicolae Steinhardt in October 1988, provides the following piquant summary: "In the end, observing this episode in retrospect, we find a comic note as well. We have the image of a tremendous machinery being unleashed (The First and Third Directorates, the Bucharest Headquarters Inspectorate and the Cluj County Inspectorate, Military Unit 0800, the Special Unit T for intercepting conversations, the special services for following ("F"), correspondence ("S"), and "111," the heavies [generals] Gianu Bucurescu, Aurelian Mortoiu, col. Gheorghe Ardeleanu the commandant of the Special Unit for Antiterrorist Warfare, etc. etc.) for *what*? To record a simple meeting between two people in which the essential element—the conversation in Steinhardt's house—slipped through their fingers [for lack of microphones in Steinhardt's residence]. A striking contradiction between effort and its results, calling to mind Kant's famous definition of laughter: *an effect arising from the sudden transformation of a tension-filled expectation into nothing*" (Ardeleanu, *N. Steinhardt*, 276, original emphasis).

37 Vatulescu, *Police Aesthetics*, 32.

38 Steinhardt, cited in Vatulescu, *Police Aesthetics*, 32.

39 Vatulescu, *Police Aesthetics*, 35.

40 This is not a property only of Securitate files but appears in bureaucratic documents from many places. For example, Doyle writes of the same feature in Guatemalan police documents, in which an agent was chastised by his superior for *not* using the passive: "'Never personify—the third person must always be used'" (Doyle, "Atrocity Files," 61).

41 Vatulescu, *Police Aesthetics*, 37.

42 Ibid., 38.

43 Ibid., 46–49.

44 Hull, *Government of Paper*, 21.

45 Poenaru, "Contesting," 219.

46 Ibid., 174.

47 For example, Kligman and Verdery, *Peasants*; Nadkarni, "Secrets and Lies"; Oushakine, "Terrifying Mimicry"; Poenaru, "Forgive Your Neighbor"; Vatulescu, *Police Aesthetics;* Yurchak, *Everything Was Forever.*

233

[48] Şerbulescu, *Monarhia*, 136, 137–38, 147.

[49] Hacking, "Making Up People."

[50] See especially the twenty-six-volume file labeled "Lectori, Doctoranzi, Studenţi—SUA" (Lecturers, Doctoral Students, Students—USA), which includes most of the anthropologists who passed through communist Romania as well as Fulbright lecturers and other scholars. ACNSAS, FD, file 12618/1-26.

[51] Tudoran, *Eu, fiul lor*, 9.

[52] Poenaru, "Contesting," 222.

[53] Ibid., 246.

[54] Ibid., 247.

[55] Poenaru, "Contesting," 252.

[56] Hull, *Government of Paper*, 127, 140.

[57] Harper, *Inside the IMF*, 11–12.

[58] There might be some sharing of documents between the Securitate and the Foreign Intelligence Service (as is clear from my own file), and documents might go to Party organs or the Ministry of Justice for penal cases, but for the most part, files produced by Securitate officers circulated only among them.

[59] Harper, *Inside the IMF*, 22.

[60] Ibid., 23.

[61] Hull, *Government of Paper*, 135.

[62] Timothy Garton Ash, in his ruminations on his Stasi file, comes to a similar conclusion. As his file forces him to ask himself what the differences are between being a spy and working sometimes secretively as a writer, he finds "disconcerting affinities between the two pursuits." If a newspaper's job is "to convey intelligence," then "I was a spy for 'intelligence'…. I was a spy for the reader" (Garton Ash, *The File*, 65).

[63] Poenaru, "Forgive Your Neighbor," 6.

[64] Ibid.

[65] Ginzburg, "Inquisitor," 157, 162. My thanks to Florin Poenaru for this reference.

[66] Malinowski, *Argonauts*, 88–90.

[67] McGranahan, personal communication; see her *Arrested Histories*. See also Robben, "Ethnographic Seduction."
[68] Thanks to Cristina Vatulescu for this observation (see *Police Aesthetics*, ch. 5, esp. p. 164).

Chapter 2

[1] Canetti, *Crowds and Power*, 290.
[2] Weber, *From Max Weber*, 233.
[3] Nugent, "States, Secrecy," 699.
[4] Banu, "Strămoşii Securităţii," 484.
[5] The titles in the respective languages are: Komitet Gosudarstvennoi Bezopasnosti, Ministerium für Staatssicherheit, Departamentul Securităţii Statului, Államvédelmi Osztály or Államvédelmi Hatóság, Urząd Bezpieczeństwa or Służba Bezpieczeństwa.
[6] See Pierre Bourdieu's discussion of "having an opinion" in his *Distinction*, 399–401.
[7] Lochrie, *Covert Operations*, 1.
[8] Bok, *Secrets*, 5–6.
[9] Ibid., 8.
[10] Special thanks to Phyllis Mack for her help with this argument.
[11] Corbeanu, *Amintirile*, 258.
[12] Ibid., 237–38.
[13] There are other ways of carving into this enormous topic. For African ethnography, for example, Piot gives four general directions of analysis: structural-functionalist, which emphasizes secrecy's political alliances and the educational role of initiation societies; Marxist, which examines it as a means of social control in a system of power relations; Freudian, which sees it as a way of dealing with infantile sexuality and maturation; and semiotic, which looks at its role in systems of communication. See Piot, "Secrecy," 354. Likewise, Bok sees secrecy as containing a number of strands, relating to privacy, intimacy, silence, invisibility, prohibition, deception, and sometimes the uncanny, mysterious, or sacred (*Secrets*, 5–9).

[14] Marilyn Strathern did me the favor of saying that this comparison would not pay off, thereby challenging me to try it anyway, and then of graciously finding some virtue in the result. My thanks for both gestures.

[15] Thanks to Vlad Naumescu for discussion of this point.

[16] Nadkarni writes: "The emphasis upon uncovering hidden truths—and, indeed, making secrecy the very criterion for the validity of truth—may deflect examination of the 'truths' that are revealed. We should get away from thinking about the truth of these files" ("Secrets and Lies," 9).

[17] Given the tremendous gender disparity in both officers and informers of the Securitate, I will use the pronoun "he." Anisescu reports ("Comunicarea," 77) that the average informant was recruited between the ages of 21 and 40, male, urban, married with a family, not involved in politics; had a high school education, and was recruited from the cultural and economic environments. In the CNSAS archive, women comprise only 1.6 percent of one partial inventory of Securitate officers. Deletant's listing of the heads of the major divisions of the Securitate as of 1989 shows five women out of 48 (Deletant, *Ceaușescu*, 377–79). Both Glaeser and Gökarıksel (personal communication) have observed the same gender disproportions for the Stasi and the Polish SB, respectively. And Garton Ash reports that for the Stasi, only 10 percent of informers were women (*The File*, 123). See also Macrakis, *Seduced*, 244, who notes that most of the women on the Stasi staff were secretaries, and those recruited as agents were often used to seduce targets.

[18] Crăciun, *Zeii zilei*, 13.

[19] Banu, "Secretul de stat," 53. The minister was Chivu Stoica.

[20] Stoler, *Archival Grain*, 26.

[21] *The Law on the Defense of the State Secret in the Romanian Socialist Republic*, 17 December 1971 (Legea 23/1971), available at http://www.legex.ro/Lege-23-17.12.1971-474.aspx (accessed June 5, 2013). Note that "the state secret" always appears in the singular.

[22] Király, *Fenomenologia*, 85.

[23] Ibid., 84.

[24] Ibid., 80, 86–87.

[25] Coțoman, *Dosarele Securității*, 48.

236

[26] Szűcs, personal communication. I am indebted to Ms. Szűcs for her extended commentary on an earlier version of this chapter.

[27] "The totalitarian movements have been called 'secret societies established in broad daylight'" (Arendt, *Origins*, 376).

[28] Ibid., 435, 378.

[29] Abrahamian, "Secret Police."

[30] See, for example, Barth, *Ritual and Knowledge*; Bellman, *Language of Secrecy*; Herdt, *Secrecy*; Murphy, "Secret Knowledge," and "Kpelle Brokerage"; Piot, "Secrecy"; Tuzin, *Cassowary's Revenge*; Webster, *Primitive Secret Societies*.

[31] See Herdt, *Secrecy*.

[32] Herdt, "Secret Societies," 360–61.

[33] Murphy, "Secret Knowledge," 193.

[34] Murphy, "Kpelle Brokerage," 668–69.

[35] See Humphrey, *Karl Marx Collective*; Kligman and Verdery, *Peasants*, 189–200; Verdery, "Socialist Societies."

[36] Hazelrigg, "A Reexamination," 328.

[37] Gusterson, *Nuclear Rites*, 90.

[38] Price, *First-Time*; Bellman, *Language of Secrecy*.

[39] Urban, "Torment of Secrecy," 210.

[40] Crăciun, *Zeii zilei*, 10.

[41] This is only part of the loyalty oath sworn by officer Iosif Pall in 1954. See ACNSAS, Fond Cadre (FC), file P-126, 179.

[42] My thanks to Vlad Naumescu for a discussion relevant to the points in this paragraph. Abrahamian, "Secret Police," also writes of initiation.

[43] See, for example, the description in Negulescu, *Spionaj*, 39–44, 80.

[44] Cosma, *Cupola*, 67.

[45] Fedor, *Russia*, chapter 1.

[46] Bucur Constantin, AIO CNSAS 216; interviewed by Cristina Anisescu, 15-2-2011.

[47] Arendt (*Origins*, 403) writes of the multiplication of offices in socialism mainly within the secret police, "with its extremely complicated, widely ramified network of agents, in which one department is always

237

assigned to supervising and spying upon another. Every enterprise in the Soviet Union has its special department of the secret police, which spies on party members and ordinary personnel alike. Co-existent with this department is another police division of the party itself, which again watches everybody, including the agents of the NKVD, and whose members are not known to the rival body."

[48] Cosma, *Cupola*, 66; see also Anisescu and Moldovan, *Pseudomemoriile*, 221–22.

[49] Cosma, *Cupola*, 67, emphasis added; see also Troncotă, *Istoria*, 33.

[50] Information in this paragraph comes from Albu, *Informatorul*, and Anisescu et al., *"Partiturile" Securității*, 204–16. Recruitment involved much more nuance than I can cover here—for instance only some informers were made to sign oaths or write out the crimes that had targeted them for recruitment.

[51] Perhaps a record was the more than four years of harassment that the Hungarian secret police invested in recruiting the future Cardinal László Paskai. See Tabajdi and Ungváry, *Elhallgatott múlt*, 323–24.

[52] Anisescu et al., *"Partiturile" Securității*, 212.

[53] Garton Ash writes of Stasi informer recruits, "One of the rituals of initiation as a regular IM was to choose your own secret name" (*The File*, 15). I note that the use of pseudonyms has parallels in village practices of using nicknames for people, rather than their legal first and last names.

[54] For an example, see Anisescu et al., *"Partiturile" Securității*, 656–57. A similar oath was required of prisoners upon leaving prison, as well as of people whom the Securitate interrogated, and its effects could be durable. Vultur reports, "Some of my interlocutors had been interrogated by the Securitate and forced to sign oaths that they would tell no one about the interrogation to which they had been subjected. Forty years after these events and fourteen years after the 1989 Revolution, their self-censorship or their fear was still so great that, with the exception of one woman who told me about her interrogation in detail, not one of the other seven interlocutors had the courage to mention it" (Vultur, "Viața cotidiană," 359).

[55] Arendt, *Origins*, 392.

56 Simmel, "The Secret," 330. See also Luhrmann: "Ritualism produces, or helps to produce, the other characteristic of such groups—their construction of a second 'world,' parallel to but distinct from the mundane" (Luhrmann, "Magic of Secrecy," 159).

57 Luhrmann, "Magic of Secrecy," 141.

58 Pseudonyms usually began with letters from the target's real name, or used his/her occupation or physical characteristics. They always appeared in quotation marks and often in capital letters so they would be easy to find in the text (Chiva and Albu, *Noi și Securitatea*, 40).

59 Abrahamian, "Secret Police," 22.

60 Anisescu and Moldovan, *Pseudomemoriile*, 181.

61 Luhrmann, "Magic of Secrecy," 162.

62 ACNSAS, FI, DUI 195847/3, 213.

63 In this case, their prurience seems to have had some limits, for one could also sense a kind of prudishness: there was no mention of the target's love life—not because they could not gather any information about it, but because the target was engaging in same-sex relationships. See Tabajdi and Ungváry, *Elhallgatott múlt*, 334.

64 Instructions for those carrying out the censorship of mail, for example, specify that they must not wear their uniforms or enter any of the clubs, shops, or headquarters of the Interior Ministry (see Anisescu et al., *"Partiturile" Securității*, 367).

65 Crăciun, *Zeii zilei*, 10.

66 Coruț was a Securitate counterintelligence officer until the 1989 revolution and then became a hugely successful writer of Securitate fiction. Among his more than one hundred novels (unfortunately unavailable in English) are the popular *Octogonul* (Octagon) series, including *Quinta spartă* (Broken quintet), *Neînfrânții* (The unvanquished), (*Lumina Geto Daciei* (The light of Geto-Dacia [considered the Romanians' ancestral people]), and *Fulgerul albastru* (Blue lightning).

67 Fedor, *Russia*.

68 See, for example, George, "Dark Trembling,"; Herdt, *Secrecy*, chapter 5; Tuzin, *Cassowary*.

69 Herdt, *Secrecy*, 34.

239

[70] The information in this paragraph is from Herdt, *Secrecy*, chapter 1.

[71] Ibid., 40.

[72] For the Soviet Union, Arendt (*Origins*, 431) recalls the context of ubiquitous spying, in which everyone felt under surveillance including the police themselves; careers were very insecure, with ascents and falls every day, so each word uttered became subject to retrospective interpretation.

[73] Cosma, *Cupola*, 27–28.

[74] See Barbu, *Vin americanii!*, and Kligman and Verdery, *Peasants*, 277–78.

[75] Kligman and Verdery, *Peasants*, 145–48 and chapter 5, passim. The mountainous region of Maramureș, for instance, was crawling with people of all kinds: peasants, army deserters, children of kulaks, and so forth. The population was highly solidary with such refugees, feeding them and helping to keep them alive for extended periods, as much as five or more years. See Pop-Săileanu, 'Să trăiască partizanii,' 29.

[76] See, for example, the work of Henri Stahl (*Contribuții*) and Oana Mateescu ("Forests and Documents") on the communal-property societies of the Vrancea region, and of Gail Kligman on *Călușari* folkdance groups (*Căluș*, 19–22). My thanks to Gail Kligman for pointing out the parallels with peasant traditions and to Cosmin Budeanca for information on the partisan groups. Oana Mateescu (personal communication) contends that the Vrancea groups were not strictly speaking "secret societies" with secrecy oaths but were organized for specific property conflicts through their communal-property association (*obște*). Nonetheless, Zoltán Rostás reports learning from Henri Stahl himself that Stahl had been made to take a secrecy oath when he became a member of the Vrancea *obște* in the 1930s (personal communication).

[77] Király, *Fenomenologia*, 77–79.

[78] See Măgureanu, "Durata." Concerning the Polish UB/SB, Gökarıksel notes (personal communication) that it was fascinated with its most important competitor, the Catholic Church and especially the Vatican, in terms of (secret) communication networks. Gökarıksel spoke with an ex-informer who joked about it. "Who learned about the news way before the Communist security apparatus? The Vatican, of course. They knew everything."

[79] Getty and Naumov, *Road to Terror*, 16.

[80] This, at any rate, is the conclusion of much feminist writing after the collapse of socialism concerning gender relations during it. See, for example, Funk and Mueller, *Gender Politics*.

[81] Erickson, "Secret Societies," 195.

[82] Anikó Szűcs, personal communication. My thanks to her for raising a number of the questions I pose here.

[83] Coifescu, "O zi din viața," 11–18.

[84] Țârlescu Gheorghe, AIO CNSAS 213, Part II, 2; interviewed by Cristina Anisescu, 15-06-2011.

[85] ACNSAS, FC, file P-126.

[86] See next chapter. This being the case, I must regret that Officer Pall is the only one of my case officers whose personnel file I have access to and whose "privacy" I am hereby violating. I thank him for his good judgment in my case, but turnabout is fair play.

[87] ACNSAS, FC, file P-126, 39–40. In my file, I am often referred to as a tourist. An article in *Securitatea* magazine identified "tourists" as especially likely to be spies, therefore objects of special scrutiny. See Drăgoi, "Selecționarea," 30–31.

[88] Too late for inclusion in this book, I was able to meet two of my Securitate officers, who albeit cautiously, welcomed me with surprising warmth. The results of these discussions will appear in future publications.

[89] Glaeser, *Political Epistemics*, 316.

[90] Ibid., 315

[91] Ibid.

[92] Gusterson, *Nuclear Rites*, 98. See also Gary Marx, *Undercover*, 166–67, for similar conclusions concerning under-cover police work in the US.

[93] Crăciun, *Zeii zilei*, 18. For more on officers' overwork, see Anisescu and Moldovan, *Pseudomemoriile*, 213.

[94] Marius Oprea, personal communication.

[95] Ibid.

[96] Glaeser, *Political Epistemics*, 319 (emphasis added).

[97] Tabajdi and Ungváry, *Elhallgatott múlt*, 92.

241

[98] Bucur Constantin, AIO CNSAS 216; interviewed by Cristina Anisescu, 15-2-2011.

[99] Coruț, *Quinta spartă*, 13, 15.

[100] Glaeser, *Political Epistemics*, 321.

[101] Țârlescu Gheorghe, AIO CNSAS 213, Part II, 2; interviewed by Cristina Anisescu, 15-06-2011.

[102] Thanks to Cosmin Budeanca for this information.

[103] ACNSAS, FC, file P-126, 207.

[104] Law 23/1971, ART. 1: "The defense of the state secret is a patriotic duty, an obligation of all citizens of the Romanian Socialist Republic—workers, peasants, intellectuals, and other categories of working people—through which they contribute to defending the revolutionary achievements of the Romanian people, and to the independence, the sovereignty, and the territorial integrity of our state." See http://www.legex.ro/Lege-23-17.12.1971-474.aspx (accessed June 8, 2013). See also Király, *Fenomenologia*, 76–89.

[105] Lochrie, *Covert Operations*, 1.

[106] Taussig, "Transgression," 355, original emphasis. Thanks to Bruce Grant for this reference.

[107] See Gable, "Secret Shared," 227, who writes of Manjaco secrecy that secrecy/concealment "had as much to do with concealing an empty bottle as it did with hiding a full one."

[108] For a fascinating description of an instance in Hungary in which two informers fabricated a case against István Péntek, see Tabajdi and Ungváry, *Elhallgatott múlt*, 233–41. Although even the security police's legal department recognized that the case was fabricated, Péntek was condemned.

[109] Zilber, *Monarhia*, 84.

[110] Vatulescu, *Police Aesthetics*, 4–5.

[111] Taussig, "Transgression," 356.

[112] I would not want to leave the impression that this was always an officer's reaction to losing an informer. That would have varied by time, place, the officer's personality, and the informer's importance. An informer who was giving poor information of little use, as Corbeanu was, would be easier to relinquish than one who was strategically situated.

242

[113] Simmel, "The Secret," 345.

[114] ACNSAS, FD, file 3429/6, 127. It is noteworthy that when secret police organizations hastened to destroy files after the various revolutions of 1989, informer files were a high priority. The Polish film *Psy* (*Pigs*), by Władysław Pasikowski, opens with just such a scene. See also Vatulescu, *Police Aesthetics*, 31.

[115] Glaeser, *Political Epistemics*, 327.

[116] Ibid., 335.

[117] Ibid., 315–16.

[118] Tabajdi and Ungváry, *Elhallgatott múlt*, 348–60.

[119] Troncotă, *Istoria*, 133–34. This database was known as the Cartoteca.

[120] Bălan, "Preocupări," 33.

[121] Ţârlescu Gheorghe, AIO CNSAS 213, Part II, 2; interviewed by Cristina Anisescu, 15-06-2011.

[122] Galison, "Removing Knowledge," 234, emphasis added.

[123] Gross, *Revolution from Abroad*, 225–40.

[124] Foucault, "Author," 118. See also Frow, *Time*, 188–89.

[125] Horváth and Szakolczai, *Dissolution*, chapters 6 and 7.

[126] Glaeser writes, "The effective messenger of bad news is someone beyond the doubt that she might want to harm the addressee. The repeated loyalty rituals of the individual Stasi officers to the Stasi and the party, as well as the loyalty demonstrations of the Stasi as an organization to party and state, have to be seen also in this light. At least the officers felt that it was this greater unquestionable loyalty that allowed Stasi to reveal more of the bad news than, for example, the party's internal information systems" (*Political Epistemics*, 326–27).

[127] See Verdery, "Socialist Societies."

[128] Gusterson, *Nuclear Rites*, 79.

[129] Ibid.

[130] Quoted in Troncotă, *Istoria*, 96.

[131] Cosma, *Cum a fost*, 150–51. One should note, however, that after DIE General Pacepa's defection, it became common for members of the other branches to hold up the DIE as a negative example.

[132] Troncotă, *Istoria*, 34.

243

[133] Anisescu et al., *"Partiturile" Securității*, 637.

[134] Király, *Fenomenologia*, 88.

[135] Nugent, "States, Secrecy," 699.

[136] Mitchell, "State Effect," 77. See also Abrams, "Notes on the Difficulty."

[137] Thanks to Bruce Grant for this suggestion.

[138] Oprea, personal communication.

[139] Williams and Deletant, *Security*, 32.

[140] Király, *Fenomenologia*, 74.

[141] Troncotă, *Istoria*, 18.

[142] Fedor, *Russia*, Introduction.

[143] See Poenaru, "Forgive Your Neighbor," 6. Coruț's novels, like those of Ian Fleming and John Le Carré, present a world of clearly defined good and evil, but with aspects of the sacred and occult mixed in. Concerning the occult, I met a former Securitate officer now living in the US whose discourse was loaded with references to the occult, astrology, and mystical visions. Voicu provides a useful discussion of conspiratorial thinking in Romania, of a kind long associated with the Securitate (Voicu, *Zeii cei răi*).

[144] Taussig, "Transgression," 356.

[145] Mitchell, "State Effect," 91–95.

[146] de Certeau, *Mystic Fable*, 98.

[147] Nadkarni, "Secrets," 7–8

[148] Glaeser, *Political Epistemics*, 159.

[149] Ibid.

[150] Gusterson, *Nuclear Rites*, 88. "'Secret information is part of your being. It's not something you put down and it's gone,' said one scientist" (ibid., 88–89); "the taboos of secrecy penetrated his being so thoroughly that they even conditioned the reflexes of his body" (90). See also Luhrmann, "Magic of Secrecy," and Simmel, "The Secret."

Chapter 3

[1] ACNSAS, FI, DUI 195851/1, 6–12.

[2] ACNSAS, FI, DUI 195851/1, 1v–2.

[3] ACNSAS, FD, file 12618/1, 132–34. The Third Directorate (Direcţia a III-a) was the counterespionage division, and Maj. Gen. Alexie was one of the four most powerful men in the entire Securitate. It is unclear why I was not expelled, or labeled *persona non grata* and prevented from entering in future vists, like other anthropologists suspected of spying. Someone in some other government office must have decided against creating an incident around my expulsion.

[4] ACNSAS, FD, file 12618/1, 245–45v.

[5] See Harper, *Inside the IMF*, 9.

[6] See Poenaru, "Contesting," 151.

[7] For instance, Foucault, *Sexuality*, Part Four, chapter 2. See also Poenaru, who seeks to move beyond viewing the Securitate as just the instrument of repression and control and to see it instead as a productive form of applied social science, gathering knowledge ("Contesting," 151).

[8] Some commentators equate this shift with a change in the recruitment of Securitate officers, as the "brutes" of the early decades were replaced by men with university educations and "culture." Securitate officers themselves (see, for instance, Cosma, *Cupola*; Tăbăcaru, *Sindromul*) claim that the years of brutality were those in which non-Romanians—especially Jews and Hungarians—dominated the organization and that once the Party leaders replaced those elements, then kinder methods came to prevail. The self-serving nationalism of this viewpoint makes it an interesting datum.

[9] Bucur Constantin, AIO CNSAS 216; interviewed by Cristina Anisescu, 15-2-2011.

[10] Departamentul Securităţii Statului, "Caracterul," 39.

[11] Ibid., 45.

[12] Vatulescu, "In the Beginning," 12–13.

[13] Anisescu, "Comunicarea," 143.

[14] ACNSAS, FI, DUI 195851-1/6-12.

[15] ACNSAS, FD, file 12618/2, 66–68. The report at the end of that two-month stay in 1987 indicated that I had been followed for seventeen days, video installations had been used in my room for 25 days, and periodic secret searches were carried out at intervals of one or two days (ACNSAS, FI, DUI 195847/1,12).

[16] This is the reaction of the author of an unsigned article, "Mijloacele tehnice moderne folosite in spionaj [Modern technical means used in espionage]," *Buletin intern pentru aparatul securității statului* 1 (1968): 50.

[17] Ibid., 50–51.

[18] E.g., Ordinul Ministrului Afacerilor Interne al Republicii Populare Române nr. 85 și instrucțiunile privind supravegherea operativă organelor M.A.I. 1957 (Order of the Ministry of Internal Affairs of the RPR no. 85 and instructions concerning operative surveillance by the organs of the Ministry)," in Anisescu et al., *"Partiturile" Securității*, 398–426.

[19] Ibid., 417.

[20] ACNSAS, FD, file 12618-11/10.

[21] The technology could easily overwhelm the human dimension: as ex-officer Bucur commented, "Unfortunately, what I learned in school—that the informer was the principal means of Securitate work, the basic weapon of the information officer—is wrong, and now it's the telephone, and that isn't as it should be… Eavesdropping today, it's listened to automatically and you as an officer make no effort at all!" Bucur Constantin, AIO CNSAS 216; interviewed by Cristina Anisescu, 15-2-2011.

[22] "Directiva referitoare la munca cu agentura." In Anisescu et al., *"Partiturile" Securității*, 204–16.

[23] Ministerul de Interne, "Criterii privind recrutarea de informatori și colaboratori pentru munca de Securitate," 1976, 3. Available on the CNSAS website, http://www.cnsas.ro/documente/materiale_didactice/D%20008712_001_p19.pdf (accessed June 20, 2013). See also Glaeser, *Political Epistemics*, 149: "secret informants were the very backbone of Stasi operations, and countless Stasi documents, including the major guidelines governing the work of Stasi with secret informants (documents in Muller-Enbergs 1996), call them 'the main weapon in its struggle with the enemy.'"

[24] Anisescu et al., *"Partiturile" Securității*, 204–5.

25 Hulubaș, "Ce motive," 56; Anisescu, "Comunicarea," 67.

26 See, for instance, the list in Anisescu et al., *"Partiturile" Securității*, 669, of "specific means" for accomplishing operative surveillance, where "the informers' network" is first, followed by technological means, shadowing, etc.

27 See Drăgoi, "Selecționarea," 31.

28 Anisescu, "Comunicarea," 85.

29 Troncotă, *Istoria*, 89, 97. See also Albu, *Informatorul*, 17, for direct references to the recruitment plan and whether it was being met.

30 Anisescu et al., *"Partiturile" Securității*, 639. According to this concept, "the defense of state security is the cause and the task of the entire people," under the leadership of the Party and the D.S.S.

31 Glaeser (*Political Epistemics*, 540) reports the same thing for the Stasi.

32 Troncotă, *Duplicitarii*, 217.

33 A 1981 decree of the Interior Ministry gave Directorate I special prerogatives for organizing rural informers, using the local police force as intermediary (Troncotă, *Duplicitarii*, 50). See Ordinul Ministrului de Interne nr. D/00140 din 01.08.1981 privind organizarea și desfășurarea muncii informativ-operative de securitate în mediul rural, 1981, ACNSAS, FD, file 13074/29, 1–7. Available at http://www.cnsas.ro/documente/acte_normative/D%20013074_029.pdf, accessed June 20, 2013.

34 But for officers, see, for example, Cosma, *Cupola*; Crăciun, *Zeii zilei*: Pleșița, *Ochii*; Anisescu and Moldovan, *Pseudomemoriile*; for informers, see Corbeanu, *Amintirile*.

35 For a description of the different categories, see Albu, *Informatorul*, 13–26, and Anisescu,"'Partiturile' agenturii," 17–22. See Fedor, *Russia*, 48–49, for a description of a category similar to *persoana de încredere* introduced in the Soviet Union starting in 1954, a kind of informer who had no pseudonym, no file, no listing in the central register, and minimal documentation; the person reported orally, not in writing, and did not meet the officers in the usual safe houses.

36 Albu, *Informatorul*, 36.

37 Țârlescu Gheorghe, AIO CNSAS 213, Part 2,1; interviewed by Cristina Anisescu, 15-6-2011.

247

[38] Albu, *Informatorul*, 144–45.

[39] Glaeser, *Political Epistemics*, 288.

[40] Ţârlescu Gheorghe, AIO CNSAS 213, Part 2, 2; interviewed by Cristina Anisescu, 15-6-2011.

[41] Serviciul Român de Informaţii, *Cartea Albă*, vol. II, 47.

[42] All from Anisescu, "'Partiturile' agenturii," 31–34.

[43] Corbeanu, *Amintirile*, 244, 247.

[44] The Romanian word is *sincer*, which has a variety of meanings that range from "candid" to "honest" to "open-hearted" to "sincere," "transparent," "truthful," and "unfeigned."

[45] Albu, *Informatorul*, 128.

[46] Anisescu, "Comunicarea," 122.

[47] Ibid., 166.

[48] In Securitate files, the names of informers—usually pseudonyms, depending on the kind of informer—are always given in quotation marks, generally in capital letters. It is peculiar that in order to write about them I have to give them pseudonyms also—that is, the name I give them is not the one in the archive, because although two of mine are willing to talk with me about their informing, they do not want to be identifiable to family and friends. In "Beniamin's" case I employ the convention of quotation marks because he appears in this book in no other guise, whereas Mariana appears not just as an informer but also as a friend, in keeping with my having learned of her informing directly from her, rather than from the files, as I did with him.

[49] Banu, "Reţeaua," 12.

[50] Albu, *Informatorul*, 20. See also p. 147, for an informer "who succeeded easily in winning the confidence of his interlocutors, having a numerous entourage."

[51] Crăciun, *Zeii zilei*, 23.

[52] Anisescu, "Comunicarea," 162.

[53] A signed informer agreement from the Securitate archive specifies, "I agree not to discuss with anyone, regardless of how close a relative they may be, about the informing I will do" (Albu, *Informatorul*, 71). Corbeanu, in his memoir, reports having been instructed as follows:

"I would not tell anyone what happened this afternoon, at any price. I would not talk with anyone about my collaboration with the Securitate or leave any written trace except for the notes I would hand over to my officer personally" (*Amintirile*, 234). He did tell his mother what had happened to him when he returned very late following his lengthy recruitment meeting, but never discussed it with her again (235).

54 Anisescu, "Comunicarea," 167–68.

55 Especially interesting is Mariana's language for trying to recuperate her relations from the Securitate: a religious one [of confession and absolution] that will bring her back from "them" to "us."

56 Corbeanu, *Amintirile*, 327.

57 Albu, *Informatorul*, 50.

58 Ibid., 173.

59 Ibid., 57, 60.

60 See Vatulescu, "In the Beginning," 16.

61 Ibid., 19.

62 Tabajdi and Ungváry, *Elhallgatott múlt*, 285–311.

63 Albu, *Informatorul*, 109.

64 Vatulescu, "In the Beginning," 15.

65 Garton Ash, *The File*, 139.

66 Ibid., 115.

67 Ibid, 139.

68 Anisescu, "Comunicarea," 66, 145.

69 Albu, *Informatorul*, 135–37.

70 Ibid., 137

71 Tabajdi and Ungváry, *Elhallgatott múlt*, 256.

72 Albu, *Informatorul*, 165, 166.

73 Anisescu, "Comunicarea," 159, from ACNSAS, Fond Rețea (FR), file 590/1, 22.

74 This view, widely held among the Securitate officers in my file, is incorrect: my ancestry is Anglo-French.

75 ACNSAS, FI, DUI 195847/1, 107-107v. In this they were successful, for I renounced my village fieldwork owing to its disruption by the po-

lice, and settled on a library project for which colleagues/informers gave me a large share of the reading list.

[76] ACNSAS, FD, file 12618-2/72v.

[77] Strathern, *Gender*, 159–65.

[78] Leys, *Guilt to Shame*, 10.

[79] A great deal of research in Soviet history has called attention to the importance of personalistic ties. See, for instance, Ledeneva, *Economy of Favours*; Lovell et al., *Bribery*; and Barbara Walker's review article, "Searching," which cites additional scholars like Gerald Easter, Sheila Fitzpatrick, and others.

[80] Spufford, *Red Plenty*, 245.

[81] See, for instance, Crăciun, *Zeii zilei*, 18. From Victor Mitran, "One of the principles of this work is to follow a target as much as possible, without being observed, not so as to see what the person is doing and how he behaves, but above all to discover, where it exists, his network, his accomplices."

[82] Arendt, *Origins*, 433.

[83] Poenaru, "Contesting," 173.

[84] Vultur, "Viața cotidiană," 349–50.

[85] See Negulescu, *Spionaj*, 72. See also Anisescu et al., *"Partiturile" Securității*, 640–41 n. 2.

[86] Țârlescu Gheorghe, AIO CNSAS 213, Part 2,2; interviewed by Cristina Anisescu, 15-6-2011.

[87] Crăciun, *Zeii zilei*, 25.

[88] Hulubaș, "Ce motive," 58.

[89] Crăciun, *Zeii zilei*, 25. Sometimes a distinction is made between an informer (who reports on specific targets) and a collaborator (who reports on the atmosphere in a workplace); I have simplified by using the term "informer" for all these people.

[90] See Dumitrașcu, "Particularități," 54, 55, which observes that if informers can come with their notes written ahead of time, the meeting can be shorter, rather than the usual "up to two hours or more."

[91] See "Directiva pentru organizarea și conducerea muncii informative la sate" [Directive for organizing and carrying out informative work in

the villages], in Anisescu et al., *"Partiturile" Securității*, 220–27. See also "Directiva referitoare la munca cu agentura" [Directive referring to work with informers,] in Anisescu et al., *"Partiturile" Securității*, 204–16. For unintentionally hilarious commentary on the special problems of observing conspirativity in villages, see Dumitrașcu, "Particularități."

92 Glaeser, *Political Epistemics*, 514.

93 Anisescu, "'Partiturile' agenturii," 19 n. 14.

94 ACNSAS, FI, DUI 195851/1, 11.

95 ACNSAS, FI, DUI 195851/2, 107.

96 ACNSAS, FI, DUI 195847/1, 193.

97 —a pyrrhic victory for the recruiters, one might add. That the Securitate specialized in launching such rumors is well known. See, for instance, Neagoe-Pleșa and Pleșa, "Studiu introductiv," xx.

98 Vatulescu, *Police Aesthetics*, 50.

99 Ibid., 50, 52, original emphases. The internal quote is to a statement by Yezhov.

100 Thanks to Jan Gross for this clarification.

101 An open question concerning the Securitate's interest in networks has to do with the possibility that they may actually have been operationalizing some of the insights of network theory, much of which in fact comes from Eastern Europe. During the Cold War, scientists there had few opporunities for doing work that was not run by their governments; in consequence, they became adept at using simple computers to run simulation experiments on networks, resulting, for example, in a cheap program (still used today) for visualizing them known as *Pajek*—Slovene for "spider." (Thanks to Kirk Dombrowski for calling this possibility to my attention.) Is it too much to imagine that some of this material might have formed part of the curriculum for Securitate officers in the 1970s, when their educational level began to be raised?

102 See Verdery, *What Was Socialism*, chapter 3.

103 For instance, Securitate records from Sibiu county give ninety-eight informers aged 9 to 16 (Williams and Deletant, *Security*, 199).

104 Neagoe-Pleșa and Pleșa, "Studiu introductiv," xxiii.

105 Anisescu, "Dinamica," 38.

251

[106] A 1958 law had established this crime, but it was unevenly enforced until reiterated by decree 408 in 1985. Law 23 of 1971 regarding the protection of state secrets was also an important tool for controlling Romanians' relations with foreigners.

[107] The figures were provided on different occasions to members of Romania's Parliament by the Securitate's successor organization, the Romanian Information Service (SRI). There are many obstacles to arriving at a plausible figure. First, the previous figure available from the Securitate itself in 1986 had been 263,000 informers. Did that figure reflect informers active only in 1986, with 486,000 referring to some longer time span? If the 486,000 figure is correct, it would mean a remarkable growth of the informer network in only 3 years—but given the regime's perception of the threat from dissidents and irredentist-nationalist elements in the late 1980s, perhaps this growth did occur. Second, the requests for figures after 1989 came from the Senatorial Commission on Abuses of the Securitate; thus, inflating the participation of the general population might have seemed tactically desirable. In 1993-94 when the figures were provided, the SRI had begun to redress the precipitous decline in the status of the Securitate, which had left former officers slinking about trying to evade their former targets. By then it was becoming clear that there would not be witch-hunts of former officers. Nonetheless, at that time the SRI did not enjoy the lofty position of its predecessor and might have been somewhat more likely to present realistic figures to the Parliamentary request than would have been true of its parent organization. Third, different figures may refer to different understandings of "informer," since a number of different names/categories had existed at different times. People entered and left the network, as new ones were recruited and others lost opportunities for informing or abandoned their work. Finally, because Party members might be used as informers but were never registered as such, we have no idea how numerous such persons may have been. Some people who agreed to provide information refused to be registered as informers (see, for instance Albu, *Informatorul*, 34); others may have been registered improperly, such as the many thousands of school-children a researcher discovered who had been left out of the formal to-

tals (Anisescu, personal communication). In brief, these figures are highly provisional.

[108] Bruce, "Access," 100.

[109] Deletant, *Ceaușescu*, 380.

[110] Terry Martin describes a similar motive in the 1920s and early 1930s for increasing the use of "information activists" and unpaid informers at the expense of paid under-cover officers in the Soviet Union (Martin, *Politics*, chapter 1, 93–94). See also Williams and Deletant (*Security*, 32), who write concerning the Czechoslovak StB that fiscal austerity prevented recruiting more officers, thus a large informer network was required.

[111] I noted in my Introduction that unlike the Stasi and most other East European intelligence services, the Securitate had ceased to be fully integrated into the KGB as of about 1965. Olaru and Herbstritt report (*Stasi și Securitatea*, 13) that whereas Stasi work was always doubled by the KGB, that of the Securitate was independent. Perhaps this required a leaner budget.

[112] Foucault, *Discipline*, 3.

[113] Readers who find me too sympathetic to informers might consult István Rév's marvelous and subtle piece "The Man in the White Raincoat."

Chapter 4

[1] Former officer Bucur observed in his CNSAS interview, for example, "These days they listen to telephones all over the place, the SRI above all."

[2] His employer, a man whom Walmart hires as a consultant, is writing a book on how people buy.

[3] See *New York Times*, April 9, 2013, A1, A3.

[4] *New York Times*, February 5, 2012, Sunday Review, 7.

[5] Information based on personal communication from a colleague in that department.

[6] Feb 5, 2012, Sunday Review, 7.

[7] I presented a number of pages from my file to a close friend who had been under surveillance on my account and who had always assumed the Securitate were an active presence. As he began to read, he stopped

and said emotionally, "My heart is beating so fast I can't go on. I had *no idea* it was this bad."

8 See *New York Times*, April 7, 2013, B4, and April 8, 2013, A17.

9 Masco, "Sensitive but Unclassified," 447. See his note 4, for further references on this.

10 See *Washington Post*, July 21, 2010. "Inside the locations are employees who must submit to strict, intrusive rules. They take lie-detector tests routinely, sign nondisclosure forms and file lengthy reports whenever they travel overseas. They are coached on how to deal with nosy neighbors and curious friends. Some are trained to assume false identities." The other two articles were on July 19 and 20, by the same authors.

11 See Priest and Arkin, "Hidden World," and Masco, "Sensitive but Unclassified."

12 Priest and Arkin, "Hidden world."

13 Ibid.

14 My "sample" for this conclusion is multiple reports in the *New York Times* and on National Public Radio for the two weeks after the scandal erupted.

15 See Masco, "Sensitive but Unclassified," Goldstein, "Critical Anthropology," and Unger, *Emergency State.*

Bibliography

Abrahamian, Levon. "The Secret Police as a Secret Society." *Anthropology and Archeology of Eurasia* 32 (1993-94): 12–31.

Abrams, Philip. "Notes on the Difficulty of Studying the State." *Journal of Historical Sociology* 1 (1988): 58–89.

Albu, Mihai. *Informatorul: Studiu asupra colaborării cu Securitatea* [The informer: a study of collaboration with the Securitate]. Iași: Polirom, 2008.

Anisescu, Cristina. "Comunicarea conspirativă în rețeaua informativă a securității: Aspecte psiho-sociale" [Conspirative communication in the Securitate's informer network: psycho-social aspects]. Ph.D. diss, Alexandru Ioan Cuza University (Iași, Romania), 2011.

———. "Dinamica de structură și rol a rețelei informative în perioada 1948–1989" [The dynamics of structure and role in the informers' network in the period 1948–1989]. In *Arhivele Securității* [Securitate archives], edited by Marian Stere, 10–50. Consiliul Național pentru Studierea Arhivelor Securității, Bucharest: Editura Pro Historia, 2002.

———. "'Partiturile' Agenturii [The 'scores' of the informer network]." In *"Partiturile" Securității: Directive, ordine, instrucțiuni (1947–1987)* [The Securitate's "scores": directives, orders, and instructions, 1947–1987], edited by Cristina Anisescu, Silviu B. Moldovan, and Mirela Matiu, 16–43. Bucharest: Nemira, 2007.

———, and Silviu B. Moldovan, eds. *Pseudomemoriile unui general de Securitate* [Pseudo-memoirs of a Securitate general]. Bucharest: Humanitas, 2007.

———, Silviu B. Moldovan, and Mirela Matiu. *"Partiturile" Securității: Directive, ordine, instrucțiuni (1947–1987)* [The Securitate's "scores": directives, orders, and instructions, 1947–1987]. Bucharest: Nemira, 2007.

Ardeleanu, George. *N. Steinhardt și paradoxurile libertății* [N. Steinhardt and the paradoxes of liberty]. Bucharest: Humanitas, 2009.

Arendt, Hannah. *The Origins of Totalitarianism*. New York: Harcourt, Inc., 1968 [1951].

Bădescu, Ilie. "Frica și comunismul: Contribuții asupra Revoluției din

Decembrie" [Fear and communism: contributions on the December Revolution]. *Sociologie românească*, 1-2 (1990): 31–48.

Bakhtin, Mikhail M. *Discourse in the Novel*. In *The Dialogic Imagination: Four Essays*, edited by Michael Holquist. Austin: University of Texas Press, 1981.

Bălan, Ion, Lt. col. "Preocupări pentru întărirea vigilenței, conspirativității și compartimentării în munca de Securitate" [Preoccupations concerning the tightening of vigilance, conspirativity, and compartmentalization in the work of the Securitate]. *Securitatea* 37 (1977): 32–34.

Banu, Florian. "Rețeaua informativă a Securității în anii '50: Constituire, structură, eficiență" [The Securitate informers' network in the 1950s: constitution, structure, effectiveness]. *Caietele CNSAS* 1 (2008): 7–38.

———. "Secretul de stat în România populară sau despre societatea ermetică" [The state secret in People's Romania, or concerning the hermetic society]. *Dosarele Istoriei* 10 (2003), (Buletin C.N.S.A.S., 4): 52–54.

———. "'Strămoșii' Securității: Structuri de poliție politică din România în perioada 23 august 1944 – 30 august 1948" [The Securitate's 'ancestors': structures of the political police in Romania in the period 23 August–30 August 1948]. In *Clipe de viață. Comandorul dr. Ilie Manole la 60 de ani* [Moments of life. For Commander Dr. Ilie Manole at 60], edited by Aurel Pentelescu and Gavril Preda, 456–84. Ploiești: Editura Karta-Graphic, 2007.

Barbu, Bogdan. *Vin americanii!: Prezența simbolică a Statelor Unite în România Războiului Rece 1945–1971* [The Americans are coming! The symbolic presence of the United States in cold war Romania, 1945–1971]. Bucharest: Humanitas, 2006.

Barth, Fredrik. *Ritual and Knowledge among the Baktaman of New Guinea*. New Haven: Yale University Press, 1975.

Bellman, Beryl L. *The Language of Secrecy: Symbols and Metaphors in Poro Ritual*. New Brunswick, NJ: Rutgers University Press, 1984.

Berezin, Mabel. *Making the Fascist Self: The Political Culture of Interwar Italy.* Ithaca, NY: Cornell University Press, 1997.

Bok, Sissela. *Secrets: On the Ethics of Concealment and Revelation.* New York: Pantheon, 1982.

Bourdieu, Pierre. *Distinction: A Social Critique of the Judgement of Taste.* Cambridge, MA: Harvard University Press, 1984.

Bruce, Gary. "Access to Secret Police Files, Justice, and Vetting in East Germany since 1989." *German Politics and Society* 26 (2008): 82–111.

Buck-Morss, Susan. *Dreamworld and Catastrophe: The Passing of Mass Utopia in East and West.* Cambridge, MA: MIT Press, 2000.

Canetti, Elias. *Crowds and Power.* New York: Farrar, Strauss, Giroux, 1962.

Carpen, Paul. "Continuitate" [Continuity]. *Vitralii—Lumini și umbre: Revista veteranilor din Serviciile Române de Informație* 2 (2011): 23–24.

de Certeau, Michel. *The Mystic Fable.* Chicago: University of Chicago Press, 1992.

Chiva, Carmen, and Mihai Albu. *Noi și Securitatea: Viața privată și publică în perioada comunistă, așa cum reiese din tehnica operativă* [We and the Securitate: Private and public life in the communist period as seen from eavesdropping technology]. Pitești: Editura Paralela 45, 2006.

Coifescu, Vasile. "O zi din viața unei echipe de filaj" [A day in the life of a shadowing team]. *Vitralii—Lumini și umbre: Revista veteranilor din Serviciile Române de Informație* 2 (2011): 11–18.

Corbeanu, Nicolae. *Amintirile unui laș* [Recollections of a coward]. Bucharest: Albatros, 1998.

Coruț, Pavel. *Quinta spartă* [Broken quintet]. Np, ALTPublica, 2012 (ebook edition).

Cosma, Neagu. *Cum a fost posibil? Cârtița Pacepa* [How was it possible? Pacepa the mole]. Bucharest: Editura PACO, n.d.

———. *Cupola: Securitate văzută din interior. Pagini de memorii* [The Cupola: The Securitate as seen from inside. Memoirs]. Bucharest: Editura Globus, 1994.

257

Coțoman, Gheorghe. *Dosarele Securității: Dezvăluirile unui anchetător de la Direcția VI-a D.S.S.* [The Securitate files: revelations of an interrogator from the 6th department of the D.S.S.]. Craiova: Editura Obiectiv, 1999.

Crăciun, Ioan. *Noi am fost zeii zilei: Povestea unui fost ofiter de Securitate, ajuns victima aparatului pe care l-a slujit* [We were the gods of the day: the story of a former Securitate officer, victimized by the apparatus he served], second edition. Bucharest: EUBEEA, 2000.

Davis, Natalie Zemon. *Fiction in the Archives: Pardon Tales and Their Tellers in Sixteenth-Century France.* Stanford, CA: Stanford University Press, 1987.

————. *The Return of Martin Guerre.* Cambridge, MA: Harvard University Press, 1983.

Deák, István. "Scandal in Budapest." *New York Review of Books* 53 (October 19, 2006), http://www.nybooks.com/articles/archives/2006/oct/19/scandal-in-budapest/, accessed August 20, 2013.

Deletant, Dennis. *Ceaușescu and the Securitate: Coercion and Dissent in Romania, 1965–1989.* Armonk, NY: M. E. Sharpe, 1995.

Departamentul Securității Statului. "Caracterul științific al activității de securitate desfășurate pentru cunoașterea, prevenirea și contracararea oricăror acțiuni ostile, a faptelor și fenomenelor care pot genera sau favoriza comiterea de infracțiuni împotriva securității statului" [The scientific character of the Securitate's activity carried out for the knowledge, prevention, and counteracting of all hostile actions, facts and phenomena that might generate or favor the commission of infractions against state security]. Bucharest: Ministerul de Interne (brochure), 1989.

Dinescu, Mircea. "Cold Comfort." In *Exile on a Peppercorn: The Poetry of Mircea Dinescu*, translated by Andrea Deletant and Brenda Walker. London and Boston: Forest Books, 1985.

Dobre, Florica, ed. *Securitatea: Structuri—cadre, obiective și metode, vol. 2 (1967–1989)* [The Securitate: Structures—cadres, objectives and methods]. Bucharest: Editura Enciclopedică, 2006.

Doyle, Kate. "The Atrocity Files: Deciphering the Archives of Guatemala's Dirty War." *Harper's Magazine*, December 2007: 52–64.

Drăgoi, Victor. "Selecţionarea elementelor duşmănoase din rîndul cetăţenilor străini" [Sorting out enemy elements among foreign citizens]. *Buletin intern pentru aparatul Securităţii statului* 1 (1968): 30–34.

Dumitraşcu, Alexandru. "Particularităţi ale întîlnirilor cu informatorii din mediul rural" [Particularities of meetings with informers in the villages]. *Buletin intern pentru aparatul Securităţii statului* 1 (1968): 52–57.

Erickson, Bonnie H. "Secret Societies and Social Structure." *Social Forces* 60 (1981): 188–210.

Fedor, Julie. *Russia and the Cult of State Security: The Chekist Tradition from Lenin to Putin*. New York: Routledge, 2011.

Foucault, Michel. *Discipline and Punish: The Birth of the Prison*. New York: Pantheon Books, 1977.

———. *The History of Sexuality, Volume 1: An Introduction*. New York: Random House, 1978.

———. "What Is an Author?" In *The Foucault Reader*, edited by Paul Rabinow, 101–20. New York: Pantheon Books, 1984.

Frow, John. *Time and Commodity Culture: Essays in Cultural Theory and Postmodernity*. Oxford: Clarendon, 1997.

Funk, Nanette, and Magda Mueller, eds. *Gender Politics and Post-Communism: Reflections from Eastern Europe and the Former Soviet Union*. New York: Routledge, 1993.

Gable, Eric. "A Secret Shared: Field work and the Sinister in a West African Village." *Cultural Anthropology* 12 (1997): 213–33.

Galison, Peter. "Removing Knowledge." *Critical Inquiry* 31 (2004): 229–43.

Garton Ash, Timothy. *The File: A Personal History*. New York: Vintage Books, 1997.

George, Kenneth M. "Dark Trembling: Ethnographic Notes on Secrecy and Concealment in Highland Sulawesi." *Anthropological Quarterly* 66 (1993): 230–39.

Getty, J. Arch, and Oleg V. Naumov. *The Road to Terror: Stalin and the Self-Destruction of the Bolsheviks, 1932–1939*. New Haven: Yale University Press, 1999.

Ginzburg, Carlo. 1989. "The Inquisitor as Anthropologist." In *Clues, Myths, and the Historical Method*, 156–64. Baltimore: Johns Hopkins University Press.

Glaeser, Andreas. *Political Epistemics: The Secret Police, the Opposition, and the End of East German Socialism*. Chicago: University of Chicago Press, 2011.

Goldstein, Daniel M. "Toward a Critical Anthropology of Security." *Current Anthropology* 51 (2010): 487–517.

Gökarıksel, Saygun. "Neither Immoral Opportunist nor Good Victim?: The Socialist Collaborator." Paper presented at the Association for the Study of Nationalities meeting, New York, NY, April 2012.

———. "Seeking Truth in Transparency: Facing History and Violence in 'Postsocialist' Poland." Paper presented at the American Ethnological Society meeting, Chicago, IL, November 2013.

———. "Of Truths, Secrets, and Loyalties: Political Belonging and State Building in Poland after Socialism." Ph.D. diss., City University of New York Graduate Center, 2014.

Green, Linda. *Fear as a Way of Life: Mayan Widows in Rural Guatemala*. New York: Columbia University Press, 1999.

Gross, Jan. *Revolution from Abroad: The Soviet Conquest of Poland's Western Ukraine and Western Belorussia*. Princeton: Princeton University Press, 1988.

Gusterson, Hugh. *Nuclear Rites: A Weapons Laboratory at the End of the Cold War*. Berkeley: University of California Press, 1996.

Hacking, Ian. "Making Up People." *London Review of Books* 28, August 17, 2006: 23–26.

Harper, Richard H. R. *Inside the IMF: An Ethnography of Documents, Technology and Organisational Action*. San Diego: Academic Press, 1998.

Hazelrigg, Lawrence E. "A Reexamination of Simmel's 'The Secret and the Secret Society': Nine Propositions." *Social Forces* 47 (1969): 323–30.

Herdt, Gilbert. "Secret Societies and Secret Collectives." *Oceania* 60 (1990): 360-381.

———. *Secrecy and Cultural Reality: Utopian Ideologies of the New Guinea Men's House.* Ann Arbor, MI: University of Michigan Press, 2003.

Holquist, Peter. "'Information is the Alpha and Omega of Our Work': Bolshevik Surveillance in Its Pan-European Context." *Journal of Modern European History* 69 (1997): 415–50.

Horváth, Ágnes, and Árpád Szakolczai. *The Dissolution of Communist Power.* London: Routledge, 1992.

Hull, Matthew S. *Government of Paper: The Materiality of Bureaucracy in Urban Pakistan.* Berkeley and Los Angeles: University of California Press, 2012.

Hulubaş, Constantin. "Ce motive a avut informatorul să accepte colaborarea? " [What reasons did the informer have to agree to collaborate?] *Securitatea* 36 (1976): 56–59.

Humphrey, Caroline. *Karl Marx Collective.* Cambridge: Cambridge University Press, 1983.

———. "Myth-making, Narratives, and the Dispossessed in Russia." In *The Unmaking of Soviet Life: Everyday Economies after Socialism*, 21–39. Ithaca, NY: Cornell University Press, 2002.

Hunt, Lynn. *Politics, Culture, and Class in the French Revolution.* Berkeley: University of California Press, 1984.

Ioanid, Radu. "Anatomia delațiunii." *Observatorul cultural* no. 139, October 22, 2002 (http://www.observatorcultural.ro/Numarul-139-22-Octombrie-2002*numberID_115-summary.html, accessed May 30, 2013).

———. *Dosarul Brucan: Documente ale Direcției a III-a Contraspionaj a Departamentului Securității Statului (1987–1989)* [Dossier Brucan: Documents of the Third Directorate for Counterespionage of the Department of State Security]. Iași: Polirom, 2008.

Jowitt, Kenneth. *New World Disorder: The Leninist Extinction.* Berkeley and Los Angeles: University of California Press, 1992.

Király, István V. *Fenomenologia existențială a secretului* [The existential phenomenology of the secret]. Bucharest: Editura Paralela 45, 2001.

261

Kiss, Csilla. "The Misuses of Manipulation: The Failure of Transitional Justice in Post-Communist Hungary." *Europe-Asia Studies* 58 (2006): 925–40.

Kligman, Gail. *Căluș: Symbolic Transformation in Romanian Ritual.* Chicago: University of Chicago Press, 1981.

———, and Katherine Verdery. *Peasants under Siege: The Collectivization of Romanian Agriculture, 1949–1962.* Princeton, NJ: Princeton University Press, 2011.

Klumbyte, Neringa. "Political Intimacy: Power, Laughter, and Coexistence in Late Soviet Lithuania." *East European Politics and Societies* 25 (2011): 658–77.

Knight, Amy. *How the Cold War Began: The Igor Gouzenko Affair and the Hunt for Soviet Spies.* New York: Carroll & Graf Publishers, 2005.

Kotkin, Stephen. *Magnetic Mountain: Stalinism as a Civilization.* Berkeley and Los Angeles: University of California Press, 1995.

Ledeneva, Alena. *Russia's Economy of Favours: Blat, Networking, and Informal Exchange.* Cambridge, U.K.: Cambridge University Press, 1998.

Lefort, Claude. *The Political Forms of Modern Society: Bureaucracy, Democracy, Totalitarianism.* Cambridge, MA: MIT Press, 1986.

Leys, Ruth. *From Guilt to Shame: Auschwitz and After.* Princeton: Princeton University Press, 2007.

Lochrie, Karma. *Covert Operations: The Medieval Uses of Secrecy.* Philadelphia: University of Pennsylvania Press, 1999.

Lovell, Stephen, Alena Ledeneva, and Andrei Rogachevskii. *Bribery and Blat in Russia: Negotiating Reciprocity from the Middle Ages to the 1990s.* New York: St. Martin's Press, 2000.

Luehrmann, Sonja. *Secularism Soviet Style: Teaching Atheism and Religion in a Volga Republic.* Bloomington: Indiana University Press, 2011.

Luhrmann, T.M. "The Magic of Secrecy." *Ethos* 17 (1989): 131–65.

Macrakis, Kristie. *Seduced by Secrets: Inside the Stasi's Spy-Tech World.* Cambridge, U.K.: Cambridge University Press, 2008.

Măgureanu, Virgil. "Durata și semnificația istorică a obștilor vrâncene" [The duration and historical significance of the Vrancea communal organizations]. *Vrancea: Studii și comunicări* 8–10 (1991): 185–95.

Malinowski, Bronislaw. *Argonauts of the Western Pacific*. London, G. Routledge & Sons, 1922.

Martin, Terry. *The Politics and Sociology of Information in the Soviet Union, 1918–1954*. Manuscript in progress, n.d.

Marton, Kati. *Enemies of the People: My Family's Journey to America*. New York: Simon & Schuster, 2009.

Marx, Gary T. *Undercover: Police Surveillance in America*. Berkeley and Los Angeles: University of California Press, 1988.

Masco, Joseph. "'Sensitive but Unclassified': Secrecy and the Counter-terrorist State." *Public Culture* 22 (2010): 433–63.

Mateescu, Oana. "Forests and Documents: Evidentiary Practices in Romanian Property Restitution." Ph.D. diss., University of Michigan, 2014.

McGranahan, Carole. *Arrested Histories: Tibet, the CIA, and Memories of a Forgotten War*. Durham, NC: Duke University Press, 2010.

Mitchell, Timothy. "Society, Economy, and the State Effect." In *State/Culture: State Formation after the Cultural Turn*, edited by George Steinmetz, 76–97. Ithaca, NY: Cornell University Press, 1999.

Moldovan, Silviu B. "'Partiturile' represiunii" [The "scores" of repression]," in *"Partiturile" Securității: Directive, ordine, instructiuni (1947–1987)*, edited by Cristina Anisescu, Silviu B. Moldovan, and Mirela Matiu, 82–155. Bucharest: Nemira, 2007.

Murphy, William P. "The Rhetorical Management of Dangerous Knowledge in Kpelle Brokerage." *American Ethnologist* 8 (1981): 667–85.

———. "Secret Knowledge as Property and Power in Kpelle Society: Elders versus Youth." *Africa: Journal of the International African Institute* 50 (1980): 193–207.

Nadkarni, Maya. "Secrets and Lies: 'Truth-Telling' and Transparency in Hungary's Informer Scandals." Paper presented at the Soyuz Symposium of Postsocialist Cultural Studies, Urbana, IL, March 2011.

———. "Generation and the Ethos of Transparency in Hungary's Informer Scandals." Paper presented at the Association for the Study of Nationalities meeting, New York, April 2012.

263

Nalepa, Monika. *Skeletons in the Closet: Transitional Justice in Post-Communist Europe.* Cambridge, U.K.: Cambridge University Press, 2009.

Neagoe-Pleşa, Elis, and Liviu Pleşa, "Studiu introductiv" [Introductory study]. In *Securitatea: Structuri—cadre, obiective şi metode, vol. 2 (1967–1989),* edited by Florica Dobre, v–xxvii. Bucharest: Editura Enciclopedică, 2006.

Negulescu, Victor (Gen.). *Spionaj şi contraspionaj: Din viaţa şi activitatea unui ofiţer de informaţii (amintiri, deziluzii, speranţe), 1966-1996* [Espionage and counterespionage: from the life and activity of an information officer (Recollections, disillusionments, hopes), 1966–1996]. Tîrgovişte: Editura Bibliotheca, 1999.

Niţescu, Marin. *Sub zodia proletcultismului: Dialectica puterii* [Under the sign of proletcultism: The dialectic of power]. Bucharest: Humanitas, 1995.

Nugent, David. "States, Secrecy, Subversives: APRA and Political Fantasy in mid-20th Century Peru." *American Ethnologist* 37 (2010): 681–702.

Olaru, Stejărel, and Georg Herbstritt. *Stasi şi Securitatea* [The Stasi and the Securitate]. Bucharest: Humanitas, 2003.

Oprea, Marius. *Securiştii partidului: Serviciul de cadre al PCR ca poliţie politică* [The Party's Securitate officers: the cadre service of the RCP as a political police]. Iaşi: Polirom, 2002.

———. *Moştenitorii Securităţii* [The Securitate's heirs]. Bucharest: Humanitas, 2004.

Oushakine, Serguei Alex. "The Terrifying Mimicry of Samizdat." *Public Culture* 13 (2001): 191–214.

Perrault, Gilles. *Dossier 51: An Entertainment,* translated by Douglas Parmée. London: Weidenfeld and Nicholson, 1971.

Piot, Charles. "Secrecy, Ambiguity, and the Everyday in Kabre Culture." *American Anthropologist* 95 (1993): 353–70.

Pleşiţa, Nicolae. *Ochii si urechile poporului: Convorbiri cu generalul Nicolae Pleşiţa. Dialoguri consemnate de Viorel Patrichi in perioada aprilie 1999-ianuarie 2001* [The eyes and ears of the people: Conversations with General Nicolae Pleşiţa]. [Bucharest]: Ianus Inf SRL, 2001.

264

Poenaru, Florin. "Forgive Your Neighbor as You Forgive Yourself! Archives, Religious Discourse and Scapegoating after 1989." Paper presented at the Association for the Study of Nationalities meeting, New York, April 2012.

———. "Contesting Illusions: History and Intellectual Class Struggles in (Post)socialist Romania." Ph.D. Diss., Central European University, 2013.

Pop-Săileanu, Aristina. *'Să trăiască partizanii până vin americanii': Povestiri din munți, din închisoare și din libertate* ['Long live the partisans until the Americans come': stories from the mountains, from prison, and from freedom]. Bucharest: Fundația Academia Civică, 2008.

Price, David H. "Interlopers and Invited Guests: On Anthropology's Witting and Unwitting Links to Intelligence Agencies." *Anthropology Today* 18 (2002): 16–21.

———. *Anthropological Intelligence: The Deployment and Neglect of American Anthropology in the Second World War.* Durham: Duke University Press, 2008.

Price, Richard. *First-Time: The Historical Vision of an Afro-American People.* Baltimore: Johns Hopkins University Press, 1983.

Priest, Dana, and William M. Arkin. "A Hidden World, Growing Beyond Control." *Washington Post*, July 19, 2010, A01. Available at http://projects.washingtonpost.com/top-secret-america/articles/a-hidden-world-growing-beyond-control/ (accessed 23 August, 2013).

Rév, István. "The Man in the White Raincoat." In *Past for the Eyes: East European Representations of Communism in Cinema and Museums after 1989*, edited by Oksana Sarkisova and Péter Apor, 3–35. Budapest–New York: Central European University Press, 2008.

Robben, Antonius C. G. "Ethnographic Seduction, Transference, and Resistance in Dialogues about Terror and Violence in Argentina." *Ethos* 24 (1996): 71–106.

Robin, Corey. *Fear: The History of a Political Idea.* Oxford: Oxford University Press, 2004.

Sadurski, Wojciech. *Rights Before Courts: A Study of Constitutional Courts in Postcommunist States of Central and Eastern Europe.* Dordrecht, Netherlands: Springer, 2005.

Şerbulescu, Andrei (Belu Zilber). *Monarhia de drept dialectic* [The monarchy of dialectical law]. Bucharest: Humanitas, 1991.

Serviciul Român de Informaţii. *Cartea Albă a Securităţii* [The white paper of the Securitate], vol. II. Bucharest: Serviciul Român de Informaţii, 1995.

Simmel, Georg. "The Secret and the Secret Society." In *The Sociology of Georg Simmel*, translated by Kurt Wolff, 307–76. Glencoe, IL: The Free Press, 1950.

Skidmore, Monique. "Darker than Midnight: Fear, Vulnerability, and Terror Making in Urban Burma." *American Ethnologist* 30 (2003): 5–21.

Spufford, Francis. *Red Plenty.* Minneapolis: Graywolf Press, 2012.

Stahl, Henri H. *Contribuţii la studiul satelor devălmaşe romîneşti* [Contributions to the study of Romanian communal villages], 3 vols. Bucharest: Editura Academiei Republicii Populare Romîne, 1958–1965.

Stan, Lavinia, ed. *Transitional Justice in Eastern Europe and the Former Soviet Union: Reckoning with the Communist Past.* London: Routledge, 2009.

Stoler, Ann Laura. *Along the Archival Grain: Epistemic Anxieties and Colonial Common Sense.* Princeton: Princeton University Press, 2009.

Strathern, Marilyn. *The Gender of the Gift: Problems with Women and Problems with Society in Melanesia.* Berkeley and Los Angeles: University of California Press, 1988.

Szűcs, Anikó. "Performing the Informer: State Security Files Recontextualized in the Hungarian Art World." Ph.D. diss., New York University, 2014.

Tăbăcaru, Dumitru Iancu. *Sindromul Securităţii* [The Securitate syndrome]. Bucharest: Editura PACO, n.d.

Tabajdi, Gábor, and Krisztián Ungváry. *Elhallgatott múlt: A pártállam és a belügy—A politikai rendőrség működése Magyarországon* [Silenced past: the party state and the Ministry of Interior—the operation of the political police in Hungary between 1956 and 1990]. Budapest: Corvina Kiadó és 1956-os Intézet, 2008.

Tănase, Stelian. *Elite și societate: Guvernarea Gheorghiu-Dej, 1948–1965* [Elites and society : the Gheorghiu-Dej government, 1948–1965]. Bucharest: Humanitas, 1998.

———. *Acasă se vorbește în șoaptă: Dosar și jurnal din anii tîrzii ai dictaturii* [At home they speak in whispers: File and journal from the late years of the dictatorship]. Bucharest: Compania, 2002.

———. *Cioran și Securitatea* [Cioran and the Securitate]. Iași: Polirom, 2010.

Taussig, Michael. "Transgression." In *Critical Terms for Religious Studies,* edited by Mark C. Taylor, 349–64. Chicago: University of Chicago Press, 1998.

Troncotă, Cristian. *Duplicitarii: O istorie a Serviciilor de Informații și Securitate ale regimului comunist din România, 1965–1989* [The duplicitous ones: a history of the information services and Securitate of the Romanian Communist regime, 1965–1989]. Bucharest: Editura Elion, 2003.

———. *Istoria Securității regimului comunist din România, vol 1: 1947–1964* [A history of the Securitate of the Romanian Communist regime]. Bucharest: Institutul Național pentru Studiul Totalitarismului, 2003.

Trouillot, Michel-Rolph. *Silencing the Past: Power and the Production of History.* Boston: Beacon, 1995.

Tudoran, Dorin. *Eu, fiul lor: Dosar de Securitate* [I, their son: Securitate file]. Iași: Polirom, 2010.

Tuzin, Donald. *The Cassowary's Revenge: The Life and Death of Masculinity in a New Guinea Society.* Chicago: University of Chicago Press, 1997.

Unger, David C. *The Emergency State: America's Pursuit of Absolute Security at All Costs.* New York: Penguin, 2013.

Urban, Hugh B. "The Torment of Secrecy: Ethical and Epistemological Problems in the Study of Esoteric Religious Traditions." *History of Religions* 37 (1998): 209–48.

Vatulescu, Cristina. "In the Beginning was the Missing Record: The First Pages of Soviet-Era Secret Police Files." Paper presented at the Balkan and Eastern European Kruzhok, The Humanities Center, Columbia University, October 11, 2012.

———. *Police Aesthetics: Literature, Film, and the Secret Police in Soviet Times.* Stanford: Stanford University Press, 2010.

Verdery, Katherine. In progress. *My Life as a Spy: Memoirs of a Cold War Anthropologist.*

———. "Postsocialist Cleansing in Eastern Europe: Purity and Danger in Transitional Justice." In *Socialism Vanquished, Socialism Challenged: Eastern Europe and China, 1989–2009,* edited by Nina Bandelj and Dorothy J. Solinger, 63–82. Oxford: Oxford University Press, 2012.

———. "Socialist Societies." *International Encyclopedia of the Social and Behavioral Sciences,* edited by Neil Smelser and Paul B. Baltes, 14496–500. Amsterdam: Pergamon Press, 2002.

———. *What Was Socialism, and What Comes Next?* Princeton, NJ: Princeton University Press, 1996.

Vianu, Ion. *Exercițiu de sinceritate* [Exercise in sincerity]. Iași: Polirom, 2009.

Voicu, George. *Zeii cei răi: Cultura conspirației în România postcomunistă* [The evil gods: the culture of conspiracy in post-communist Romania]. Iași: Polirom, 2000.

Vultur, Smaranda. "Viață cotidiană și supraveghere în anii 1970–1980: Dosarele de urmărire personală ca sursă memorială" [Daily life and surveillance in the years 1970-1980: surveillance files as a source of memory]. *Anuarul ICCMER* 5–6 (2010–2011): 345–63.

Walker, Barbara. "(Still) Searching for a Soviet Society: Personalized Political and Economic Ties in Recent Soviet Historiography. A Review Article." *Comparative Studies in Society and History* 43 (2001): 631–42.

Weber, Max. *From Max Weber: Essays in Sociology,* edited by H.H. Gerth and C. Wright Mills. New York: Oxford University Press, 1946.

Webster, H. *Primitive Secret Societies: A Study in Early Politics and Religion.* New York: Macmillan, 1932.

Williams, Kieran, and Dennis Deletant. *Security Intelligence Services in New Democracies: The Czech Republic, Slovakia, and Romania.* New York: Palgrave, 2001.

Williams, Kieran, Brigid Fowler, and Aleks Szczerbiak. "Explaining Lustration in Eastern Europe: A 'Post-Communist Politics' Approach." *Democratization* 12 (2005): 22–43.

Williams, Raymond. *Marxism and Literature.* Oxford: Oxford University Press, 1977.

———. *The Sociology of Culture.* New York: Schocken Books, 1982.

Yurchak, Alexei. *Everything Was Forever, until It Was No More.* Princeton: Princeton University Press, 2006.

———. "A Parasite from Outer Space: How Sergei Kurekhin Proved that Lenin Was a Mushroom." *Slavic Review* 70 (2011): 307–33.

269

Index

273

275

Nugent, David, 77, 148

O

oaths
    loyalty oaths, 95, 111, 112, 113, 237n41
    secrecy oaths, 93, 98, 99, 109, 106, 120, 130, 136, 146, 150, 177–78, 181, 238n50, 238n54, 240n76, 248–49n53
    refusal of, 181. *See also* angajament.
occult, 244n143
Okhrana, (secret police, tsarist Russia), 130, 189
Olaru, Stejărel, 230n7, 253n111
opacity,
    and state effect, 153
Oprea, Marius, 27, 43, 127, 150

P

Pacepa, Ion Mihai (Securitate General), 16, 47, 190, 227n39, 243n131
"Pajek" (spider) computer program, 251n101
Pakistan, 39, 61, 71
Pall, Iosif Grigorie (Securitate officer),
    and Verdery file, 123, 155, 164, 241n86
    personnel file of, 120–23, 130, 155, 164, 237n41,
panopticon, 209
partible persons (embedded persons), 187, 198, 202, 210. *See also* personhood
partisans, 96, 109, 124, 170, 242n104. *See also Cruce şi Spadă.*
patriarchy, and RCP 202, 205–206
patriotism, 97, 170, 242n104
    among officers, 96, 124. *See also* informers, recruitment of.
patronage, 92, 93, 115, 190, 194, 196. *See also* clientelism; personalism.
Paskai, László, Cardinal, 223n4, 238n51
Péntek, István, 242n108
Perrault, Gilles (novel *Dossier 51), 224n9*
perestroika, 18
persoane de încredere, 170, 247n35. *See also* "trustworthy people".
personalism, 146, 188-89, 190, 195
personhood, 187–88, 202. *See also* "new socialist person"; partible persons.
Piot, Charles, 235n13
"the Piteşti phenomenon", 167
Pleşa, Liviu, 206

280

Weber, Max, 77
Williams, Kieran, 150, 253n110
Williams, Raymond, 24
Wilson, Woodrow, 79
Wizard of Oz, 81
women *see* Securitate, and gender

Y

Yezhov, Nikolai Ivanovich, 167, 251n99
Yurchak, Alexei, 231n17

Z

Zilber, Belu (Herbert) (a.k.a. Andrei Şerbulescu), 31, 36, 63, 66, 134, 229n1